RECORDED VERSIONS
GUITAR

AUTHENTIC TRANSCRIPTIONS
WITH NOTES AND TABLATURE

T0066082

Music transcriptions by David Stocker

ISBN-13: 978-1-4234-5377-2
ISBN-10: 1-4234-5377-8

HAL•LEONARD®
CORPORATION

7777 W. BLUEMOUND RD. P.O. BOX 13819 MILWAUKEE, WI 53213

In Australia Contact:
Hal Leonard Australia Pty. Ltd.
4 Lentara Court
Cheltenham, Victoria, 3192 Australia
Email: ausadmin@halleonard.com.au

Visit Hal Leonard Online at
www.halleonard.com

Underclass Hero

Words and Music by Deryck Whibley and Steve Jocz

*Chord symbols reflect basic harmony.

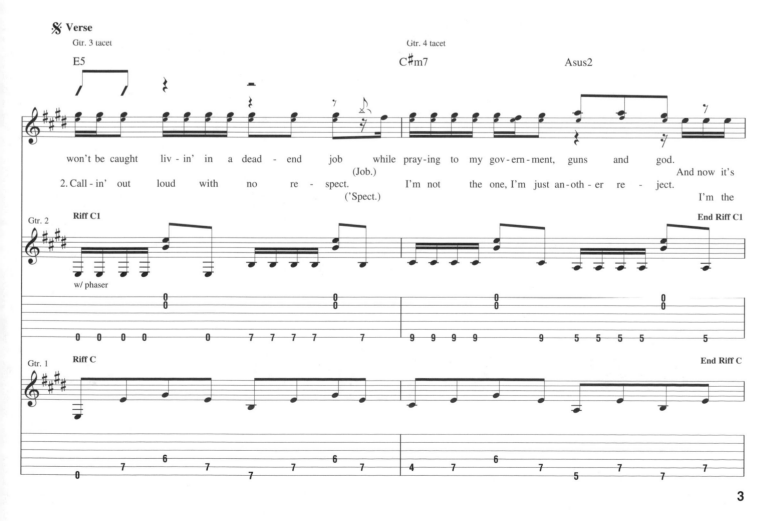

3

Gtrs. 1 & 2: w/ Riffs C & C1

us a-gainst them. We're here to rep-re-sent
voice to of-fend all those who pre-tend. Un-sung a-gainst the grain, I'm here to rise a-gainst. Now I'm

*Vol. swell

Double-time feel

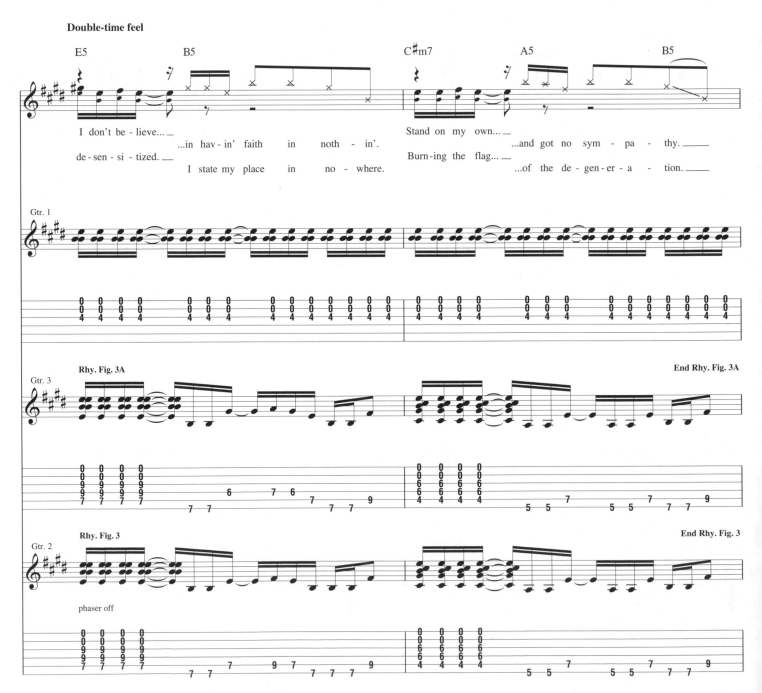

I don't be-lieve... ...in hav-in' faith in noth - in'.
de-sen-si-tized. I state my place in no - where.

Stand on my own... ...and got no sym - pa - thy.
Burn-ing the flag... ...of the de-gen-er-a - tion.

phaser off

4

Gtrs. 2 & 3: w/ Rhy. Figs. 3 & 3A
E5 B5 C♯m7 A5 B5
Wast-ing the youth... ...while be - in' young and use - less. Speak for your-self,... ...and don't pray for me. Well, be-cause
Ev - 'ry-one sing... ...the an-them of no fu - ture. Down with the mass... ...'cause we're not lis - ten - ing. Well, be-cause
Gtr. 1
P.S.
Chorus
Gtr. 1 tacet
A5 E5 B5
we're do - in' fine. And we don't need to be told that we're
Gtrs. 2 & 3
Rhy. Fig. 4
End Rhy. Fig. 4
Gtrs. 2 & 3: w/ Rhy. Fig. 4 (3 times)
A5 E5 B5 A5 E5
do - in' fine. 'Cause we won't give you con - trol. And we don't need an - y -
To Coda 1
To Coda 2
End double-time feel
B5 A5 E5 B5
thing from you. 'Cause we'll be just fine and we won't be bought and sold just like
Interlude
D.S. al Coda 1
Gtrs. 1 & 3: w/ Riffs B & B1
Gtrs. 2 & 4: w/ Rhy. Figs. 2 & 2A
E B A B E B A B
you.
(A call a-cross the un-der-class.)

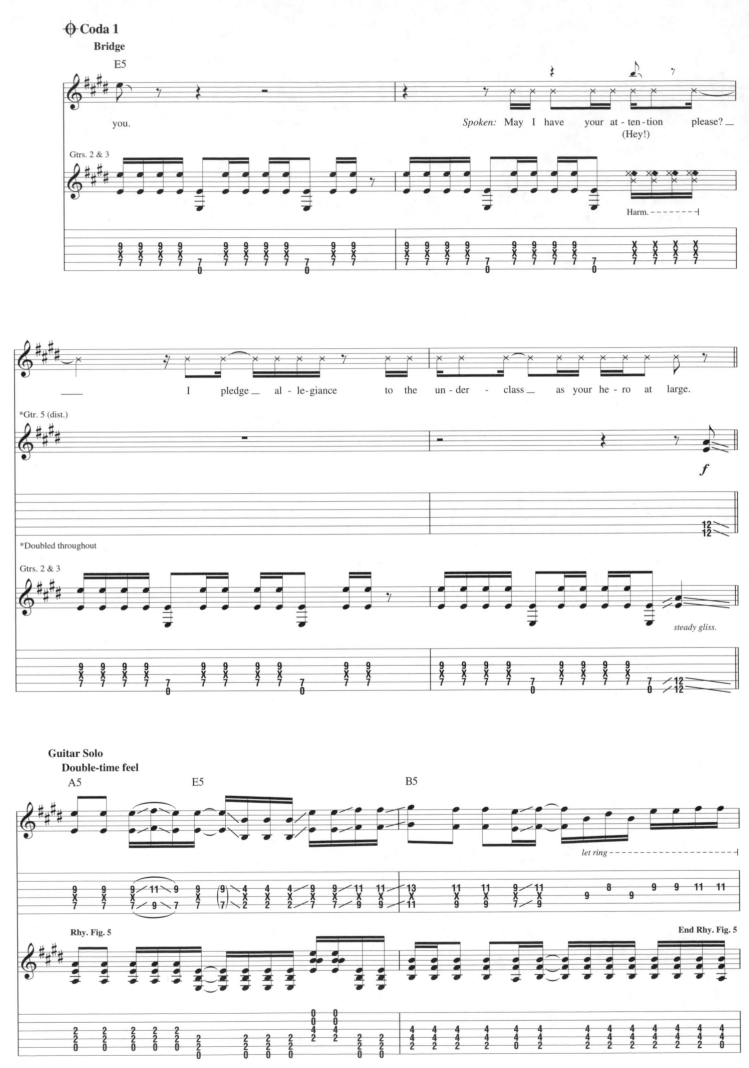

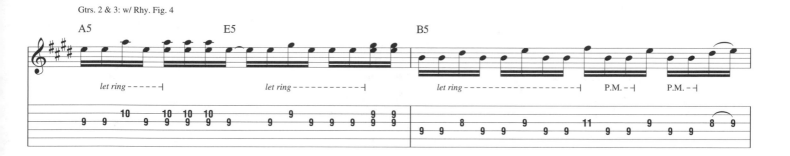

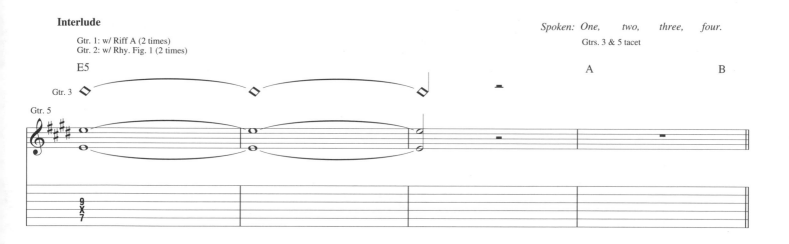

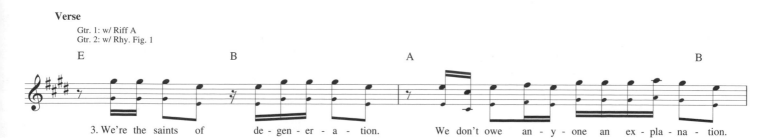

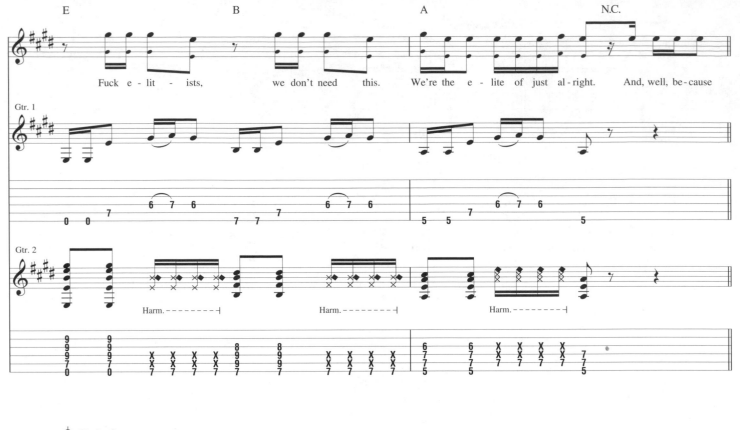

Fuck e - lit - ists, we don't need this. We're the e - lite of just al - right. And, well, be - cause

Coda 2

Outro

Gtrs. 1 & 3: w/ Riffs B & B1
Gtr. 2: w/ Rhy. Fig. 2 (1st 2 meas.)

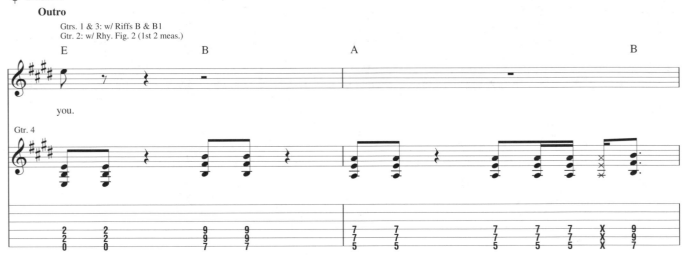

you.

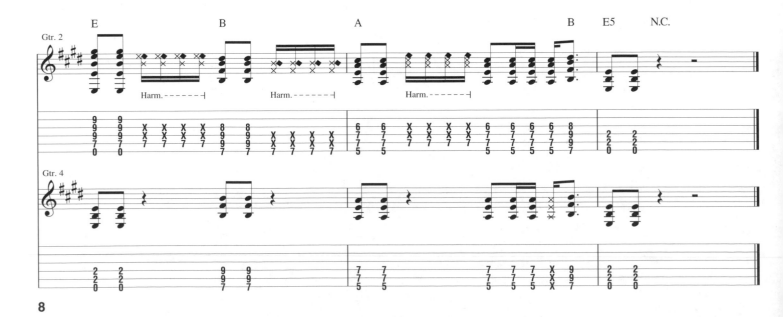

Walking Disaster

Words and Music by Deryck Whibley

*Chord symbols reflect overall harmony.

**Delay set for sixteenth-note regeneration w/ 1 repeat.
Delay signal panned hard right.

†Doubled throughout

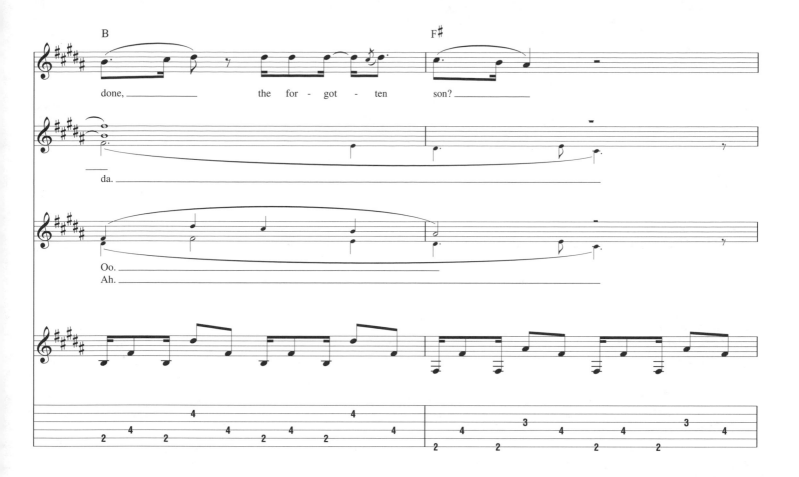

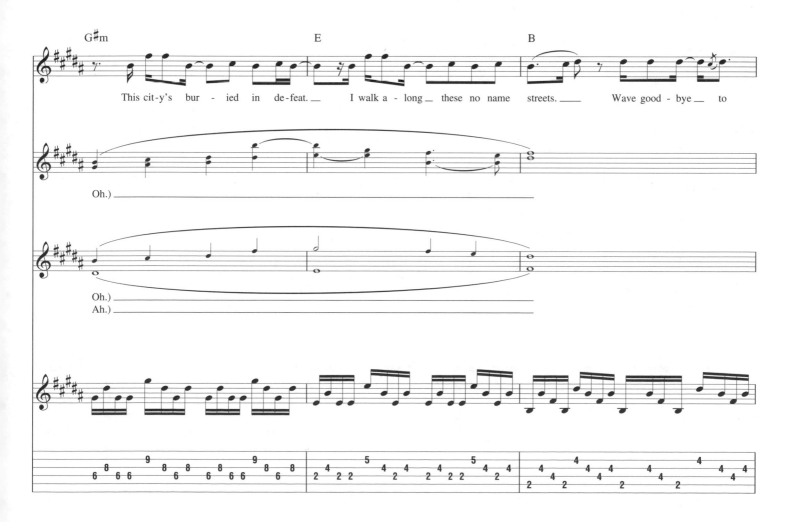

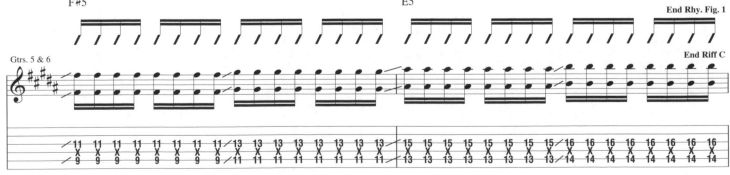

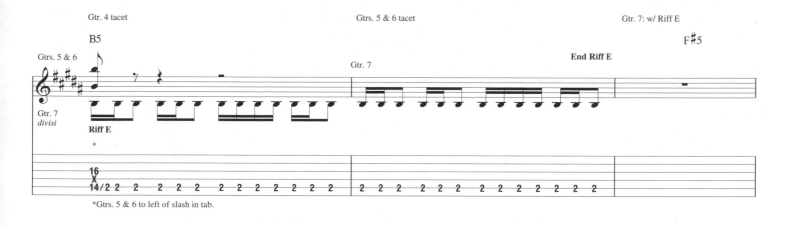

*Gtrs. 5 & 6 to left of slash in tab.

Verse

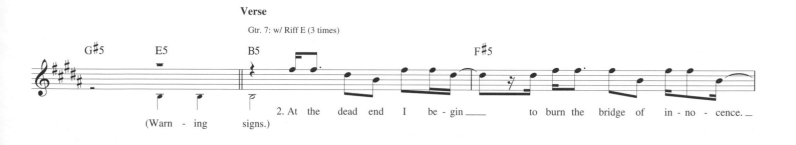

(Warn - ing   signs.)   2. At the   dead end I   be - gin ___   to burn the   bridge of   in - no - cence. ___

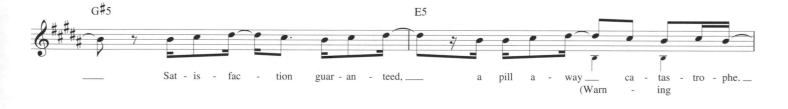

___   Sat - is - fac - tion   guar - an - teed, ___   a   pill a - way ___   ca - tas - tro - phe. ___
(Warn - ing

___   On   a   mis - sion no - where bound, ___   in - hi - bi - tions un - der - ground, ___
signs.)

𝄉 **Pre-Chorus**

Gtrs. 3 & 7 tacet

___   a   shal-low grave ___   I   have dug all by my - self.   And now   I've   been ___ gone   for
(Warn - ing   signs.)

**Sing bkgd. voc. 1st time only.

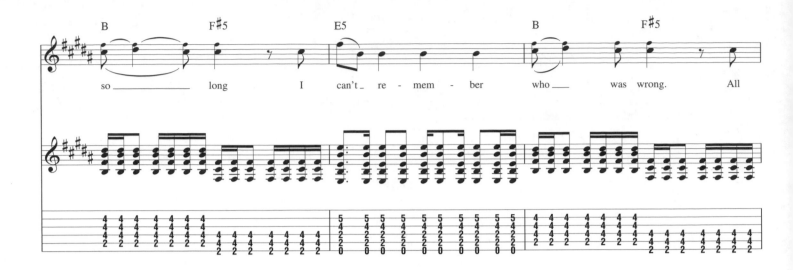

so _____ long I can't_ re - mem - ber who ___ was wrong. All

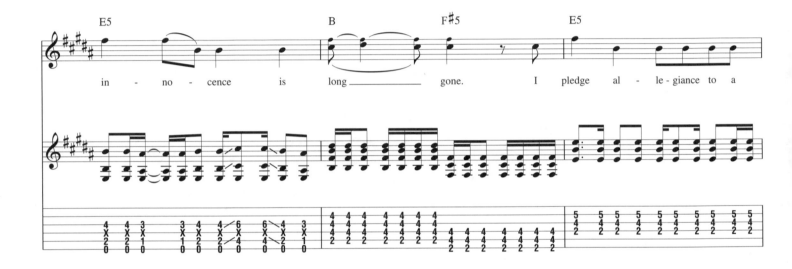

in - no - cence is long _____ gone. I pledge al - le - giance to a

Chorus

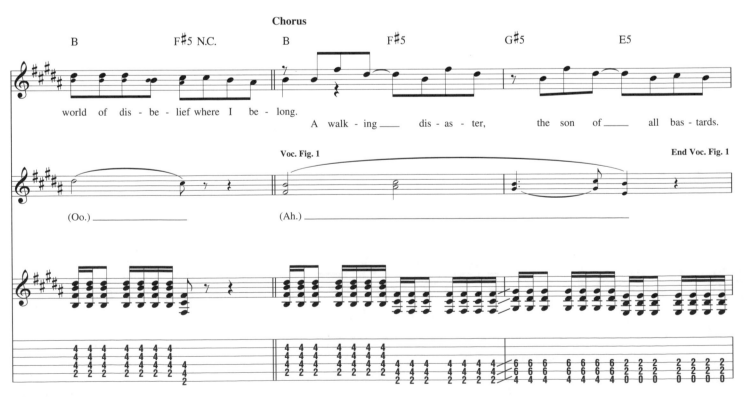

world of dis - be - lief where I be - long. A walk - ing ___ dis - as - ter, the son of ___ all bas - tards.

Voc. Fig. 1 ... End Voc. Fig. 1

(Oo.) _____ (Ah.) _____

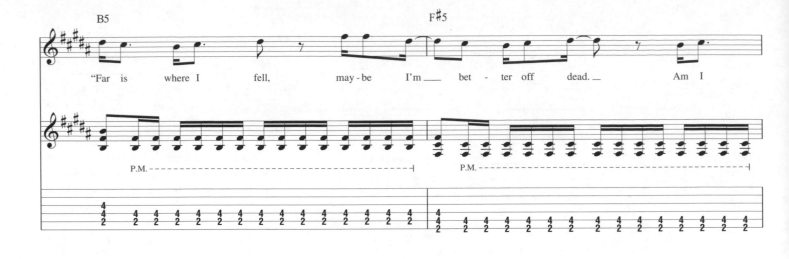

"Far is where I fell, may-be I'm ___ bet - ter off dead. ___ Am I

D.S. al Coda 1

at the end of no - where, is this as good as it gets?" ___ And now

 Coda 1

Bridge

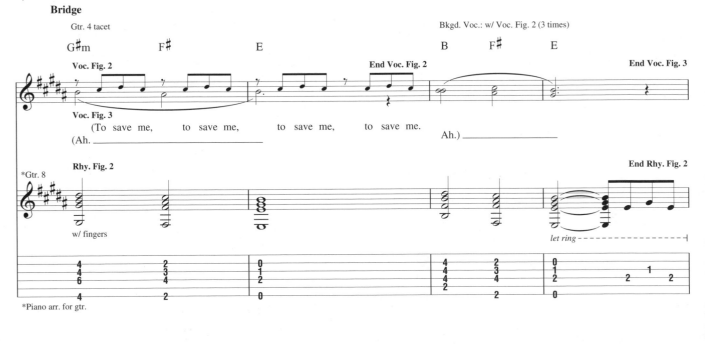

Gtr. 4 tacet

Bkgd. Voc.: w/ Voc. Fig. 2 (3 times)

Voc. Fig. 2 ... End Voc. Fig. 2 ... End Voc. Fig. 3

Voc. Fig. 3

(To save me, to save me, to save me, to save me.
(Ah. ___ Ah.) ___

*Gtr. 8 Rhy. Fig. 2 ... End Rhy. Fig. 2

w/ fingers

let ring - - - - - - - - - - - - -

*Piano arr. for gtr.

Bkgd. Voc.: w/ Voc. Fig. 3 (3 times)
Gtr. 8: w/ Rhy. Fig. 2 (3 times)

G#m   F#   E   B   F#   E   End Voc. Fig. 4

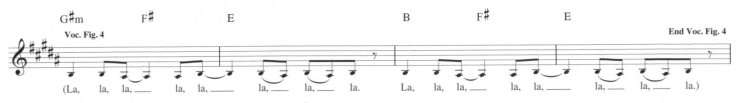

Voc. Fig. 4

(La, la, la, ___ la, la, la, ___ la, ___ la.   La, la, la, ___ la, la, la, ___ la, ___ la.)

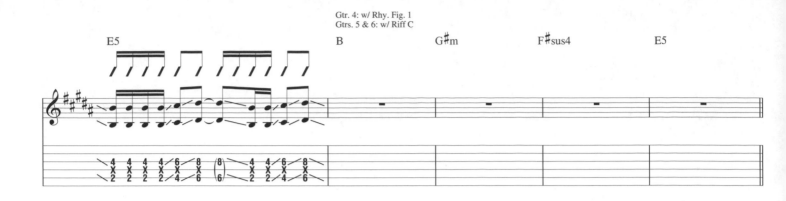

Outro-Verse
A tempo

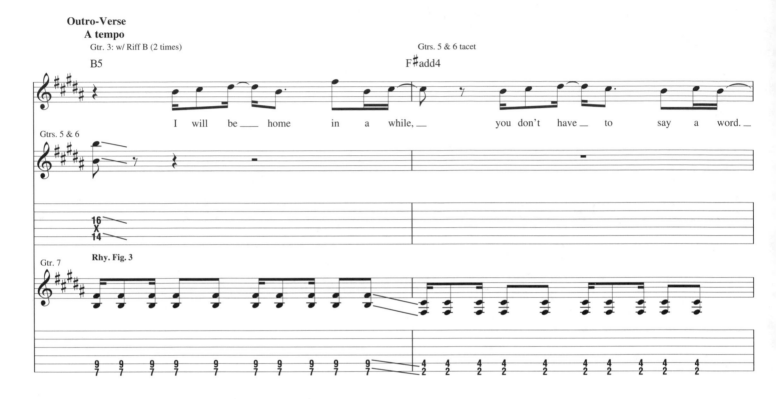

I will be ___ home in a while, ___ you don't have ___ to say a word. ___

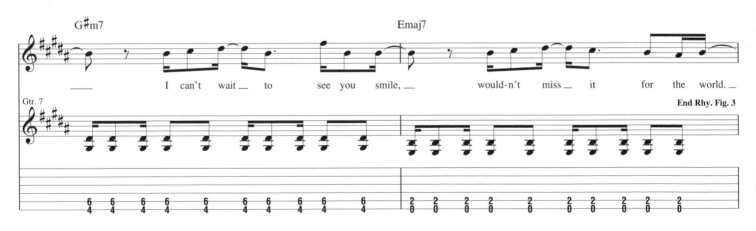

I can't wait ___ to see you smile, ___ would-n't miss ___ it for the world.

___ I will be ___ home in a while, ___ you don't have ___ to say a word. ___

___ I can't wait ___ to see you smile, ___ would-n't miss ___ it for the world.

Speak of the Devil

Words and Music by Deryck Whibley

Interlude
Gtr. 1: w/ Riff A (2 times)
Gtr. 2: w/ Riff D
Gtr. 7 tacet
** Bsus2
*** C#
B5
C#5
Riff E
End Riff E
*Gtr. 8
mf
*Elec. piano arr. for gtr.
Gtr. 6
Rhy. Fill 1
End Rhy. Fill 1
**Bass plays B.
***Bass plays C#.
Pre-Chorus
Double-time feel
Gtrs. 6 & 8 tacet
D#m
B
I've been wait - ing for the chance __ to re - u - nite __ this sick ro - mance. __
I've been wait - ing for the chance __ to nul - li - fy __ this sick ro - mance. __
Gtr. 3
F#
C#/E#
F#5
C#/E#
D#m
__ Poi - son nev - er hurt so good. So nice of you to speak of me, your clos - est
__ Pull the cord __ to det - o - nate. So sick of you, don't speak of me. The rev - 'rend

friend and en-e-my and ho-ly sav-ior of mas-o-chist. Well, it's the
saint of mis-er-y and ho-ly sav-ior of mas-o-chist. (Sub-mis-sion.)

Chorus

To Coda ⊕

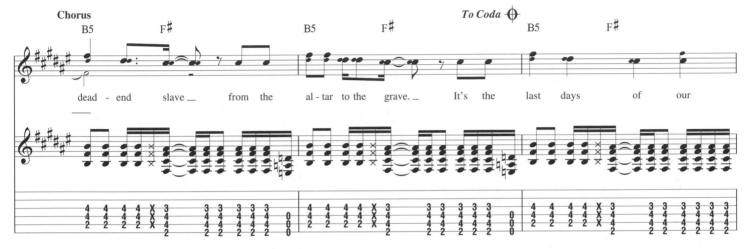

dead-end slave ___ from the al-tar to the grave. ___ It's the last days of our

End double-time feel

Gtr. 3 tacet

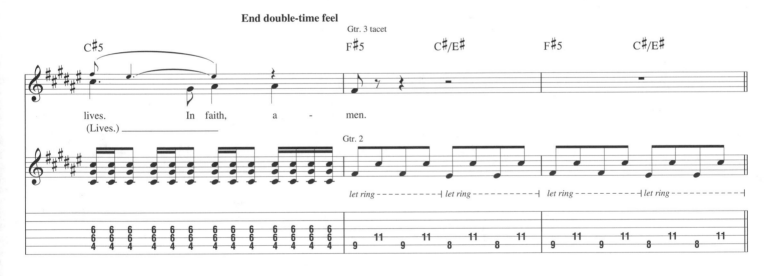

lives. In faith, a-men.
(Lives.) ___

let ring - - - - - - - | let ring - - - - - | let ring - - - - - - - | let ring - - - - - - -

Verse
Double-time feel

Gtr. 1: w/ Riff A (8 times)
Gtr. 2 tacet

Gtr. 7: w/ Riff F (7 times)

2. Time, it's been so ___ long, ___ and now there's noth-in' to say. ___ I'm try-in' so hard ___

Gtr. 7   Riff F

End Riff F

*Chord symbols reflect overall harmony.

C#sus4   F#5   D#m

to find the words to say. ___ I'm ti-red of be-ing now I'm some-thing I'm not. ___

B5   C#sus4   D#m

I can't be-lieve ___ and I nev-er thought days ___ would ___ come

B5   F#5   C#sus4

to an end. ___ Well, may-be some ___ day we'll meet a-gain. ___ If

D#m   B5   F#5

ev-er that ___ day nev-er comes ___ it ___ would be ___ too ___

D.S. al Coda

Interlude

End double-time feel

Gtr. 1: w/ Riff A (2 times)   Gtr. 6: w/ Rhy. Fill 1
Gtr. 7: w/ Riff F (2 times)
Gtr. 8: w/ Riff E

C#sus4   Bsus2   C#   B5   C#5

soon,   oh. ___

⊕ Coda

B5   F#   C#5

last days of our lives.   Well, it's the
(Lives.) ___

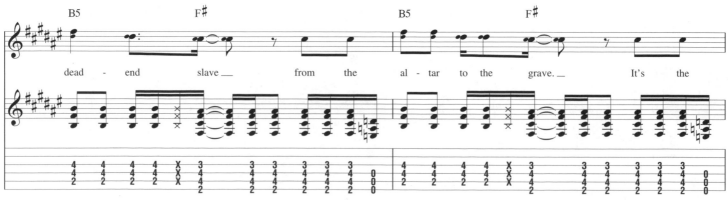

B5   F#   B5   F#

dead - end slave ___ from the al - tar to the grave. ___ It's the

Dear Father

Words and Music by Deryck Whibley

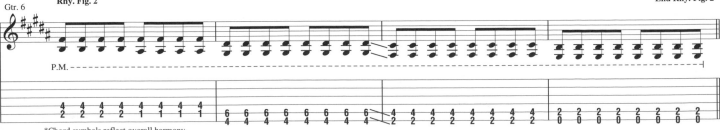

*Chord symbols reflect overall harmony.

Chorus

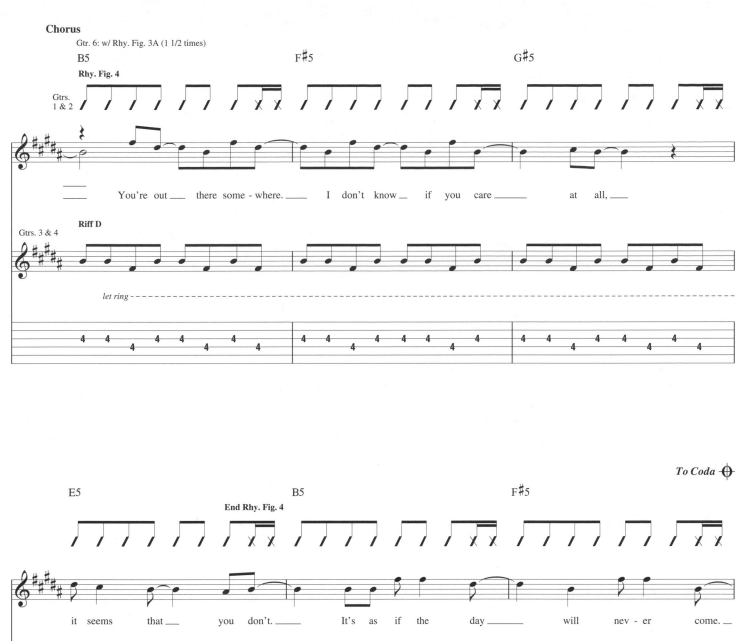

Verse

D.S. al Coda

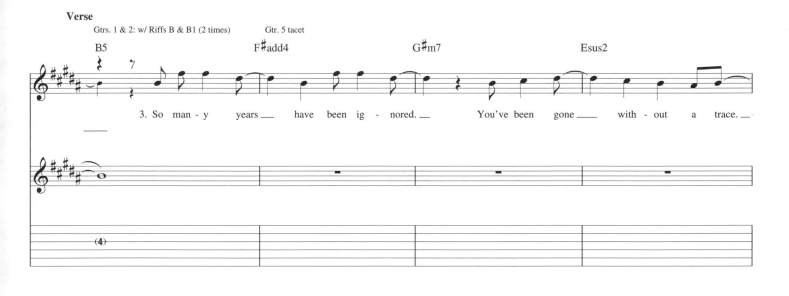

Gtrs. 1 & 2: w/ Riffs B & B1 (2 times) Gtr. 5 tacet

B5 F#add4 G#m7 Esus2

3. So man-y years have been ig-nored. You've been gone with-out a trace.

B5 F#add4 G#m7 Esus2

I'm get-ting used to know-ing you're just a name with-out a face.

Coda

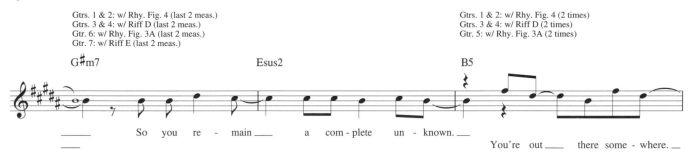

Gtrs. 1 & 2: w/ Rhy. Fig. 4 (last 2 meas.)
Gtrs. 3 & 4: w/ Riff D (last 2 meas.)
Gtr. 6: w/ Rhy. Fig. 3A (last 2 meas.)
Gtr. 7: w/ Riff E (last 2 meas.)

Gtrs. 1 & 2: w/ Rhy. Fig. 4 (2 times)
Gtrs. 3 & 4: w/ Riff D (2 times)
Gtr. 5: w/ Rhy. Fig. 3A (2 times)

G#m7 Esus2 B5

So you re-main a com-plete un-known. You're out there some-where.

Bkgd. Voc.: w/ Voc. Fig. 2

F#sus4 G#m7 Esus2

I don't know if you care at all, it seems that you don't.

Gtr. 6: w/ Riff E

B5 F#sus4 G#m7

It's as if the day will nev-er come. So you re-main

Interlude

Gtrs. 1 & 2: w/ Rhy. Fig. 4 (2 times)
Gtrs. 3 & 4: w/ Riff D (2 times)
Gtr. 6: w/ Rhy. Fig. 3A (2 times)

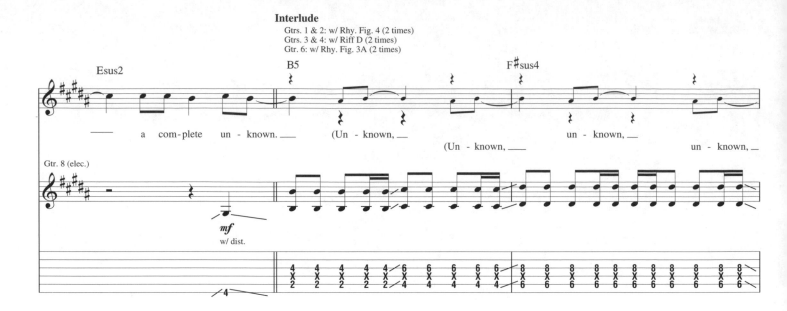

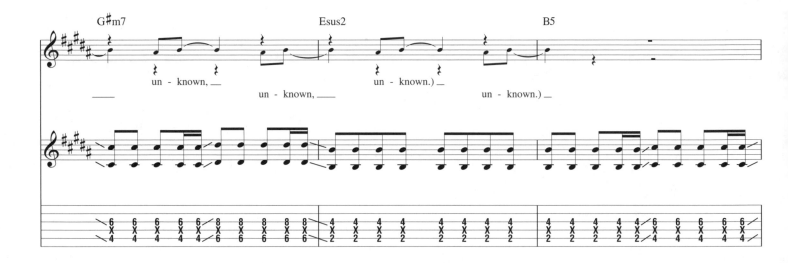

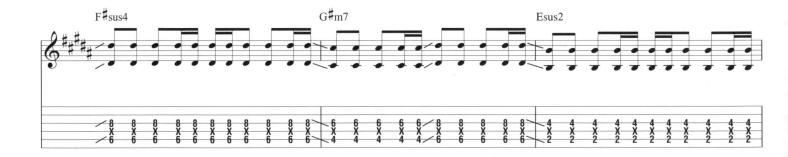

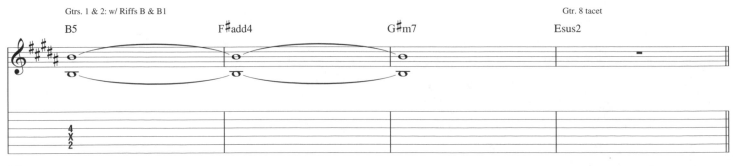

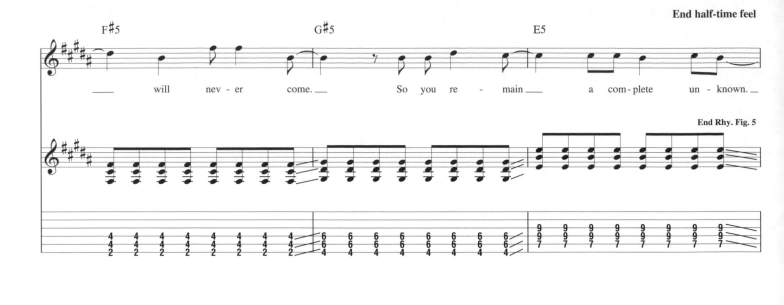

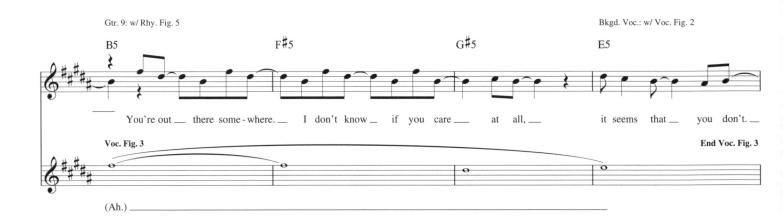

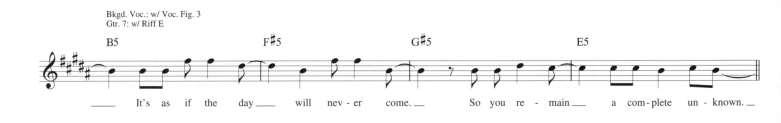

Outro

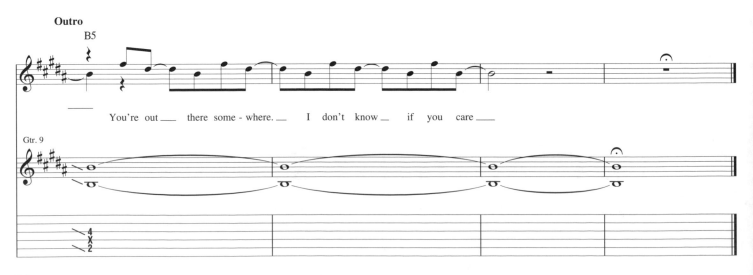

Count Your Last Blessings

Words and Music by Deryck Whibley

Gtr. 6: Tune down 2 1/2 steps:
(low to high) B-E-A-D-F#-B

Intro
Fast ♩ = 197

*Elec. piano arr. for gtr.
**Chord symbols reflect implied harmony.

***Vol. swell

Verse

Gtr. 1: w/ Riff A (2 times)
1st time, Gtrs. 2 & 3 tacet
2nd time, Gtrs. 2 & 3: w/ Rhy. Fig. 2 (1 3/4 times)

1. Last call for re- grets and de- feat, __ to fin- ish the bot- tle full of
   hands are tied and nailed to the cross, __ I'm look- ing for all the com-

Riff B
Gtr. 4 (dist.)

P.M. ----

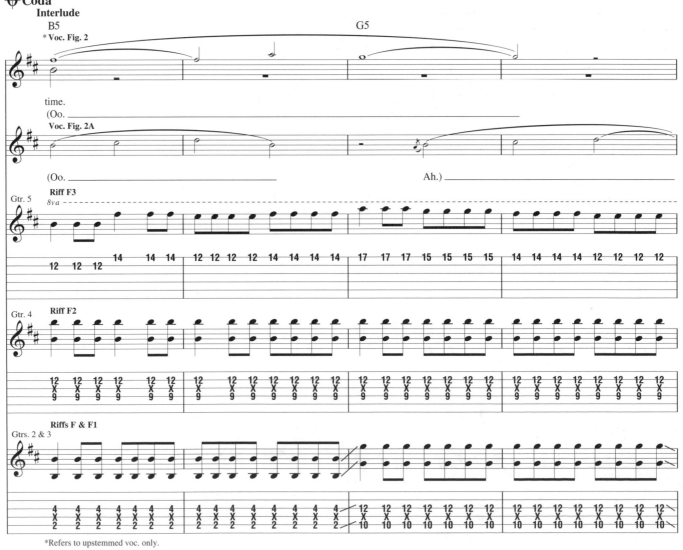

*Refers to upstemmed voc. only.

Bridge

Bkgd. Voc.: w/ Voc. Figs. 2 & 2A (2 times)
Gtrs. 2, 4 & 5: w/ Riffs F, F2 & F3 (2 times)
Gtr. 3: w/ Riff F1

I'm my own en - e - my.＿＿＿＿ I don't hear＿＿ you

*Symbols in parentheses represent chord names respective to de-tuned guitar.
Symbols above represent actual sounding chords.

Bkgd. Voc.: w/ Voc. Fig. 1 (2 times)
Gtrs. 2 & 3: w/ Riff D (2 times)

B5   D5   G5   F#5

time.

Mis - er - y's best friend can't be a dead end. A bag full of re - grets and I'm com - ing

B5   D5   G5   F#5

clean.

The self - e - lect res - i - dent re - ject. A bad hab - it, don't for - get that you bet - ter

Gtrs. 2 & 3: w/ Rhy. Fig. 1

B5   D/F#   G5   F#5

count your last bless - ings. I fell off the wag - on. I'm chas - ing six feet and now I'm run - nin' out of

Gtr. 5

Gtrs. 2 & 3: w/ Rhy. Fig. 3
Gtr. 5 tacet
Gtr. 7: w/ Riff G

B5

time.

Outro

Gtr. 1: w/ Riff A

Bm   A

Play 3 times and fade

Em   G5

Ma Poubelle

Words and Music by Deryck Whibley, Steve Jocz, Thomas Lauderdale and China Forbes

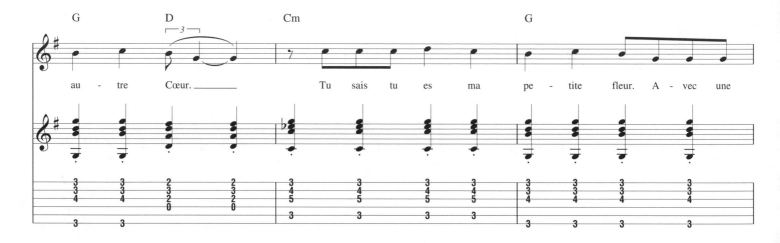

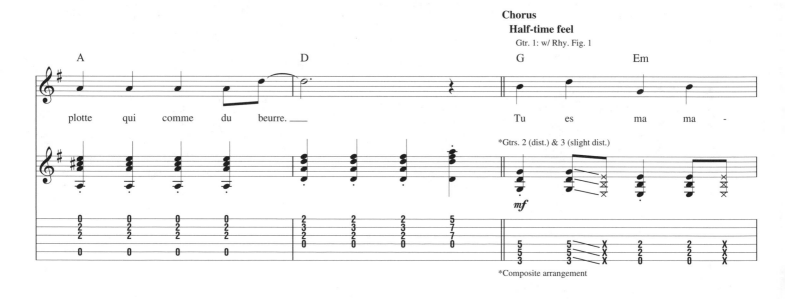

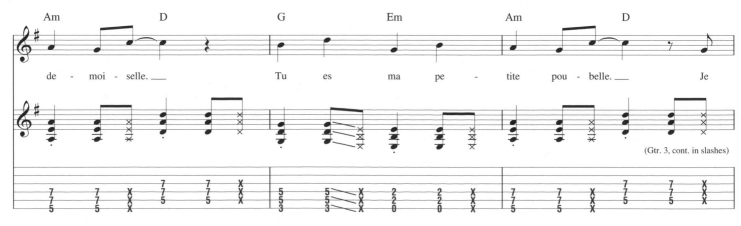

44

March of the Dogs

Words and Music by Deryck Whibley

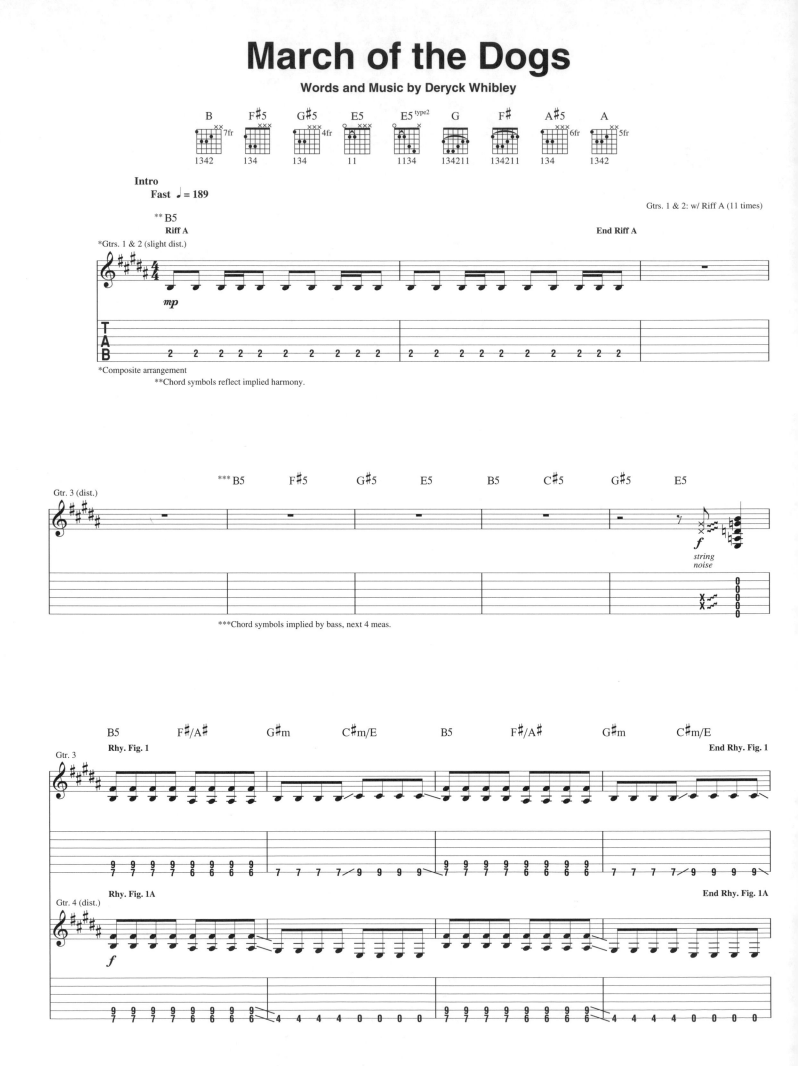

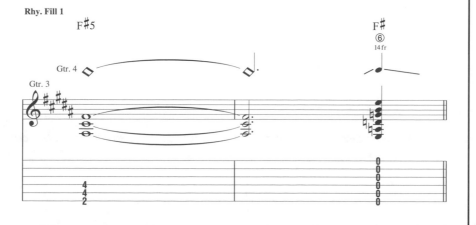

Chorus

Gtrs. 3 & 4: w/ Rhy. Figs. 1 & 1A

B5   F#/A#   G#m   C#m/E   B5   F#/A#   G#m   C#m/E

March of the dogs to a beat of dis - il - lu - sion. Sworn un - der God, breed - ing pan - ic and con - fu - sion.
The

To Coda ⊕

B5   F#/A#   G#m   C#m/E

white flag is down, send in the clowns. The car - ni - val of sins is now a - bout to be -
(Oo.) _____

Gtr. 3

Gtr. 4

Interlude

Gtrs. 3 & 4 tacet

G#m   B/F#

gin.

(Ah. _____)

*Gtr. 6 (dist.)

mf

*Doubled throughout

Gtrs. 1 & 2

w/ flanger

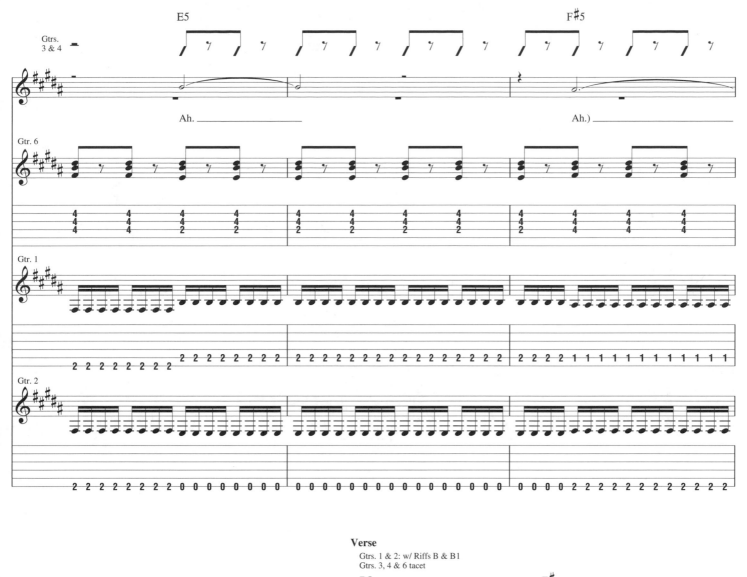

Verse

Gtrs. 1 & 2: w/ Riffs B & B1
Gtrs. 3, 4 & 6 tacet

2. It may be I'm a pes - si - mist, __

but I'd say we need an ex - or - cist.____ The root of all____

D.S. al Coda

____ e - vil stand - ing tall un - der God____ and a - bove us

Gtr. 3

Gtr. 4

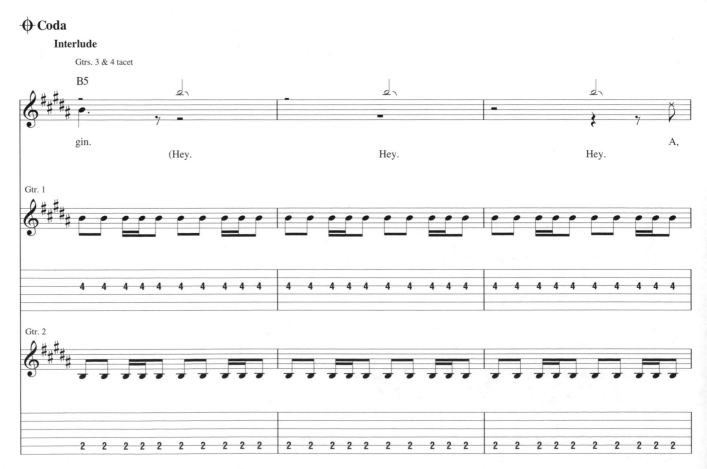

⊕ Coda

Interlude

Gtrs. 3 & 4 tacet

gin. (Hey. Hey. Hey. A,

Gtr. 1

Gtr. 2

Guitar Solo

Gtrs. 1 & 2 tacet

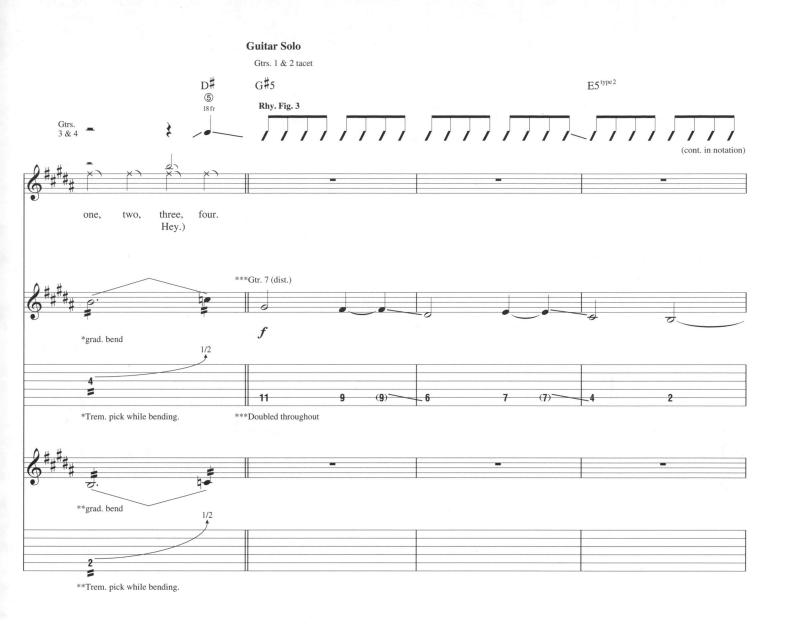

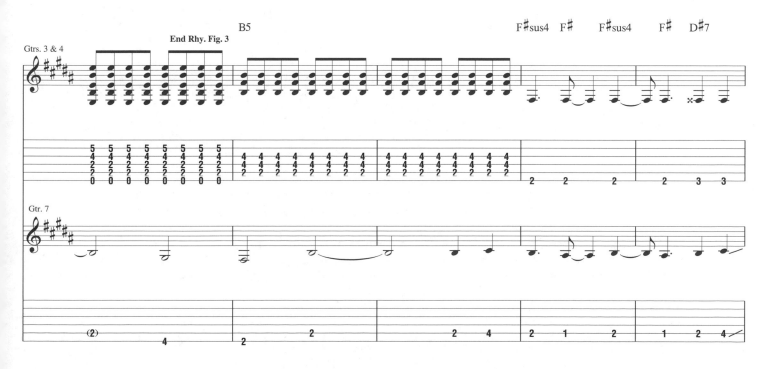

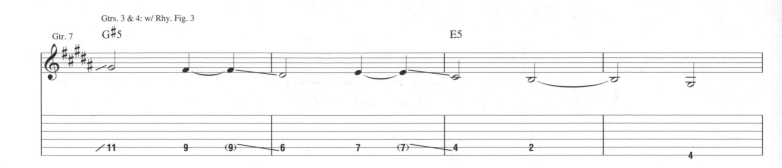

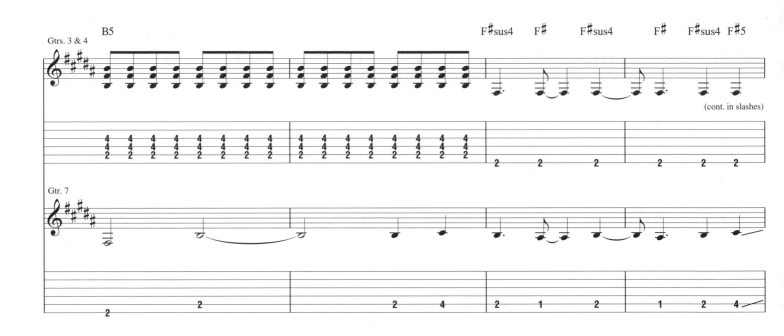

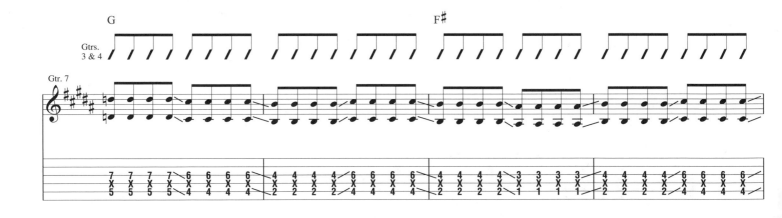

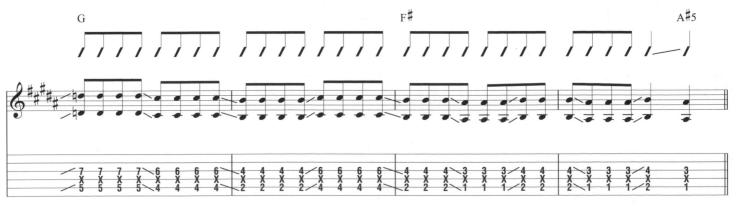

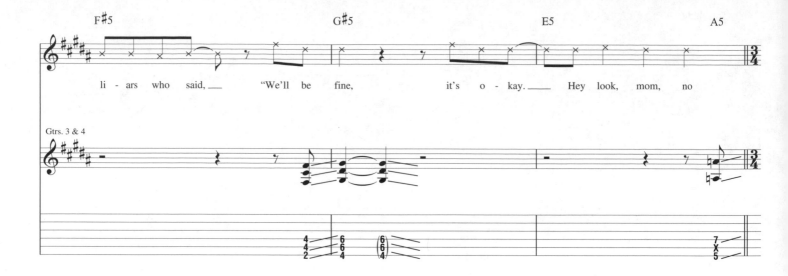

F#5　　　　　　　　G#5　　　　　　　　　E5　　　　　　　　A5

li - ars who said, __ "We'll be fine, it's o - kay. __ Hey look, mom, no

Gtrs. 3 & 4

Outro

w/ Lead Voc. ad lib. (next 15 meas.)

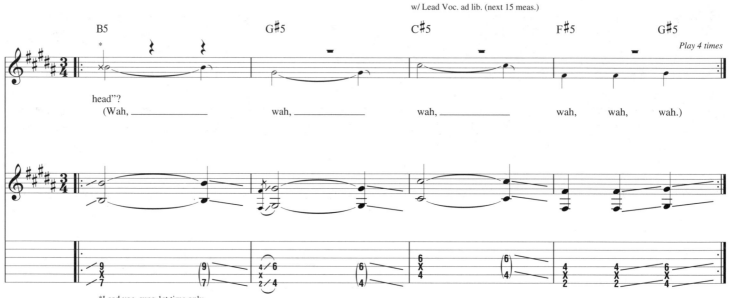

B5　　　　　　　　G#5　　　　　　C#5　　　　　　F#5　　　　G#5

Play 4 times

head"?
(Wah, _____ wah, _____ wah, _____ wah, wah, wah.)

Lead voc. sung 1st time only.

Free time

Bkgd. Voc.: w/ shouting

B5

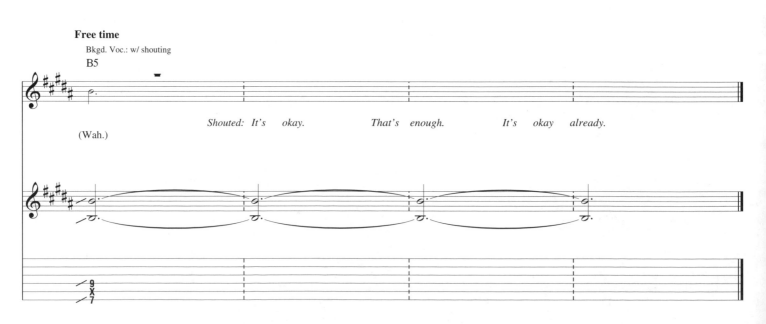

Shouted: It's okay.   That's enough.   It's okay already.

(Wah.)

The Jester

Words and Music by Deryck Whibley

blood, I'm a - lone stand - ing still. Un - der God, you can fi - re at ___ will. ___
(Like a chil - i up his ass.)

§ Chorus

Gtr. 1 tacet

___ And when the dev - il's an - gels ___
(One, two, And three, when four! When!)

Gtr. 2 (elec.)

f
w/ dist.
Harm. -
*
(cont. on lower staff)

Pitch: E
*Harm. located approx. three-tenths the distance between the 2nd & 3rd frets.

Gtr. 3 (elec.)
**Gtrs. 2 & 3
Rhy. Fig. 1

f
w/ dist.
P.S.

**Composite arrangement

___ come, take your life ___ and lead you to the flames ___ be -

Gtrs. 2 & 3
End Rhy. Fig. 1

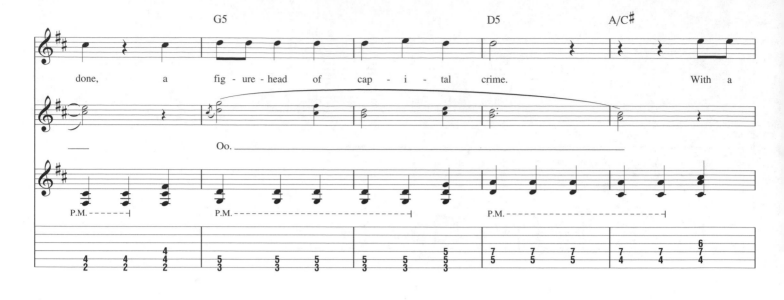

done, a fig - ure - head of cap - i - tal crime. With a

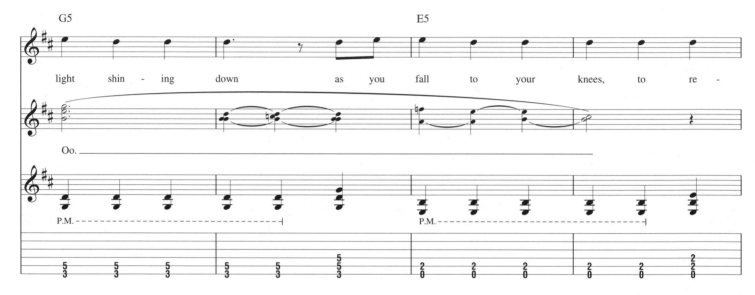

light shin - ing down as you fall to your knees, to re -

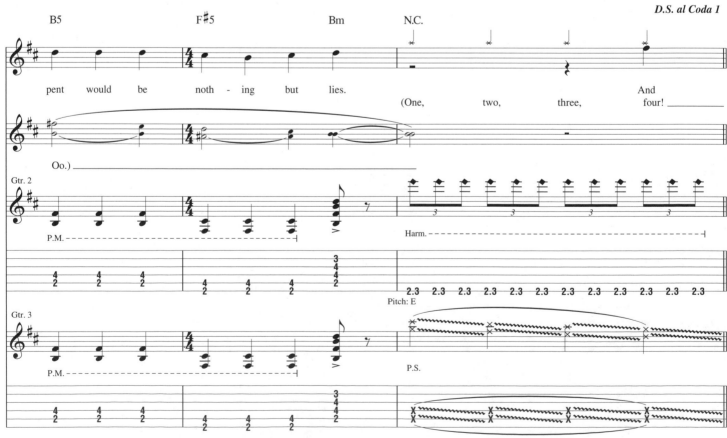

D.S. al Coda 1

pent would be noth - ing but lies.

(One, two, three, And four!

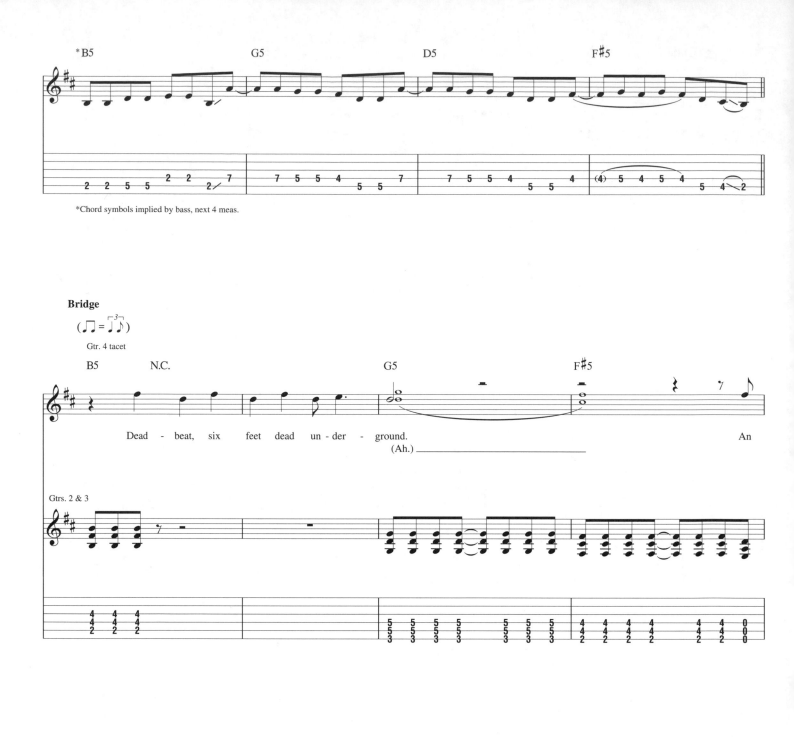

*Chord symbols implied by bass, next 4 meas.

Bridge

Gtr. 4 tacet

Dead - beat, six feet dead un - der - ground. An

(Ah.)

Gtrs. 2 & 3

D.S. al Coda 2

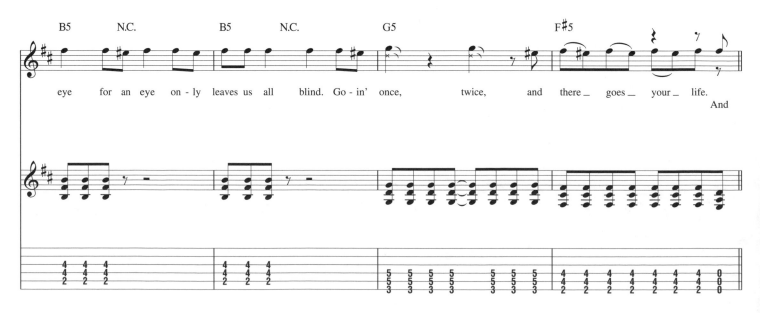

eye for an eye on - ly leaves us all blind. Go - in' once, twice, and there goes your life. And

⊕ Coda 2

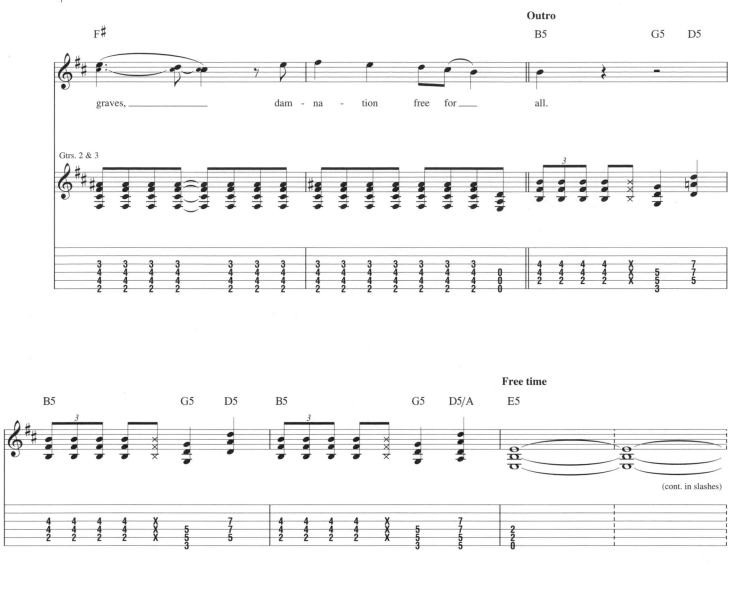

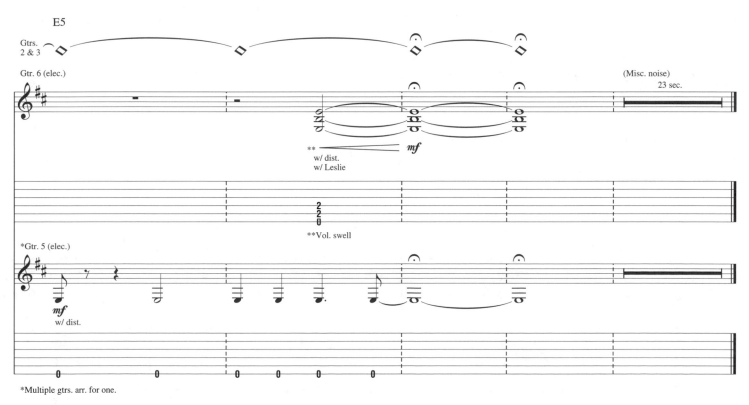

*Multiple gtrs. arr. for one.

With Me

Words and Music by Deryck Whibley

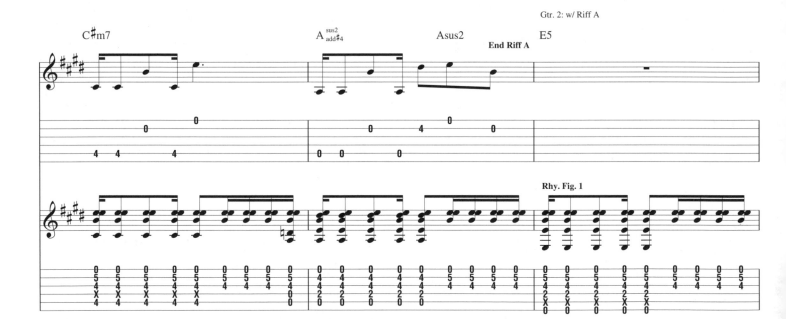

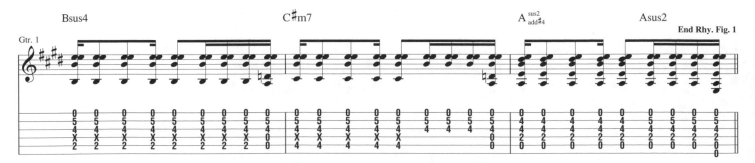

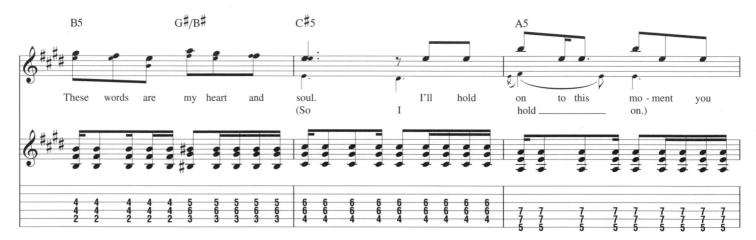

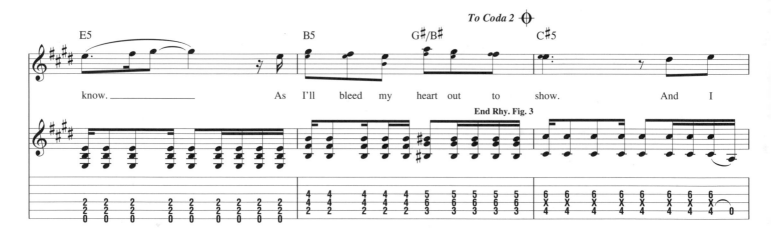

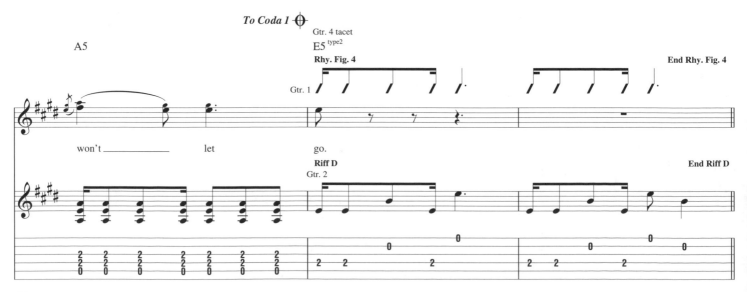

with no - where to go ____ have come to an end. ____ I want you to

Coda 1

Gtr. 1: w/ Rhy. Fig. 4
Gtr. 2: w/ Riff D

E5

Bridge

A5/E

Rhy. Fig. 5

Gtr. 4

go. In front of your

Gtr. 4

*Gtr. 6 (elec.)

(cont. in slashes) w/ dist.

*Doubled throughout

E5 type3 B5/F# C#5 B5

eyes, it falls from the skies when you don't know what you're look - ing to

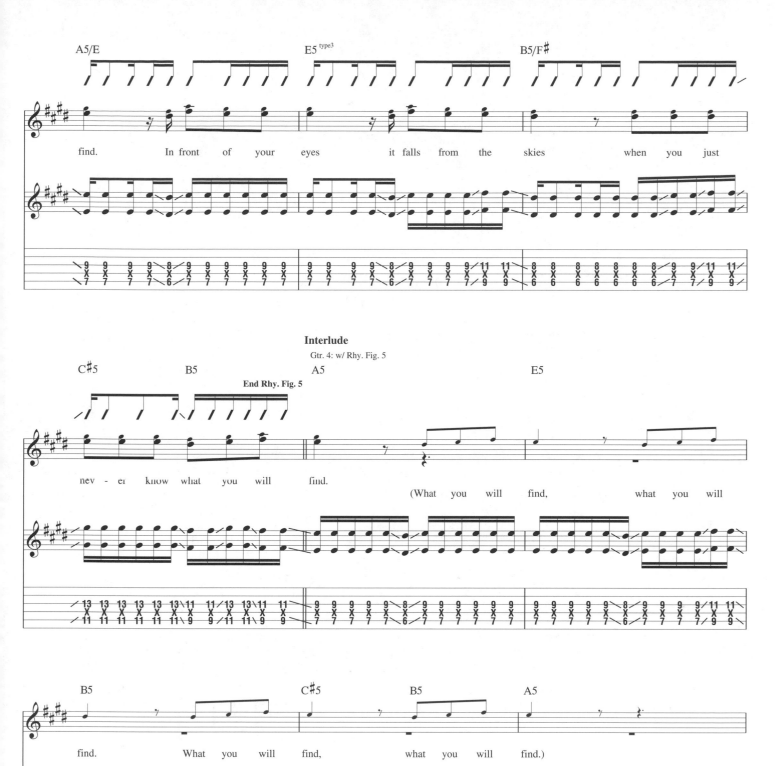

find. In front of your eyes it falls from the skies when you just

Interlude
Gtr. 4: w/ Rhy. Fig. 5

nev - er know what you will find.

(What you will find, what you will

find. What you will find, what you will find.)

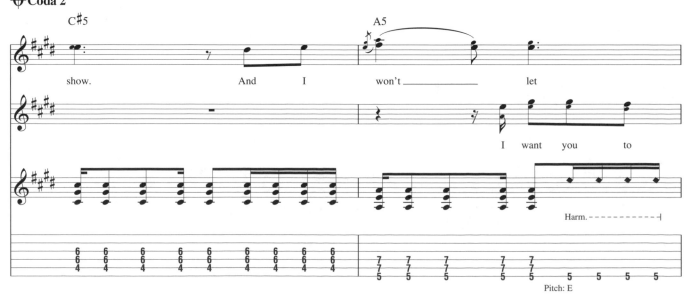

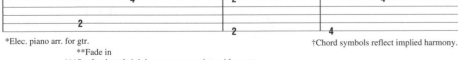

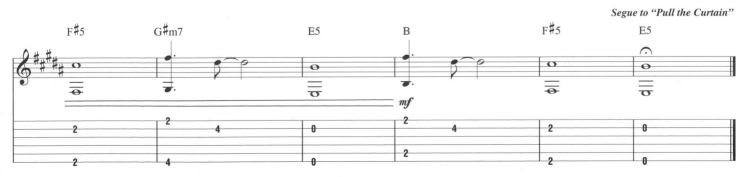

Pull the Curtain

Words and Music by Deryck Whibley

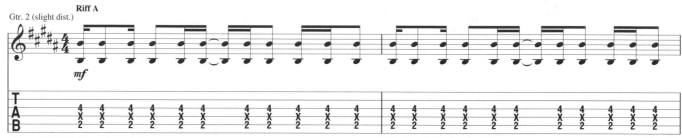

Gtr. 8: Tune down 1/2 step:
(low to high) Eb-Ab-Db-Gb-Bb-Eb

Intro

Moderately fast ♩ = 116

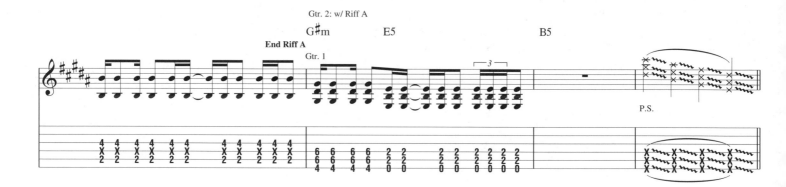

*Doubled throughout.

**Chord symbols reflect implied harmony.

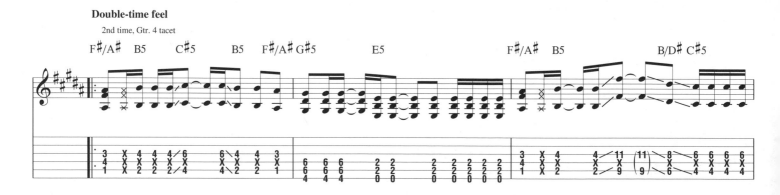

Double-time feel

2nd time, Gtr. 4 tacet

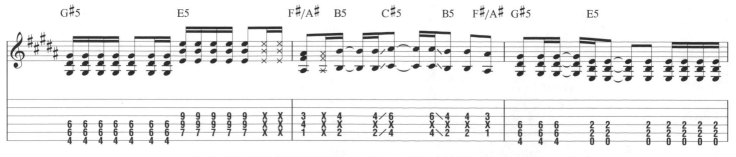

Chorus

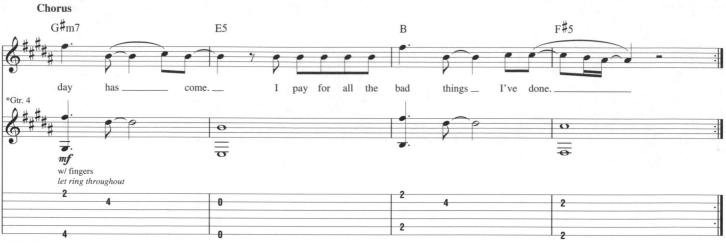

day has _____ come. ___ I pay for all the bad things ___ I've done. ___

*Gtr. 4

mf
w/ fingers
let ring throughout

*Piano arr. for gtr.

Bridge

Gtr. 4 tacet

**Voc. Fig. 1

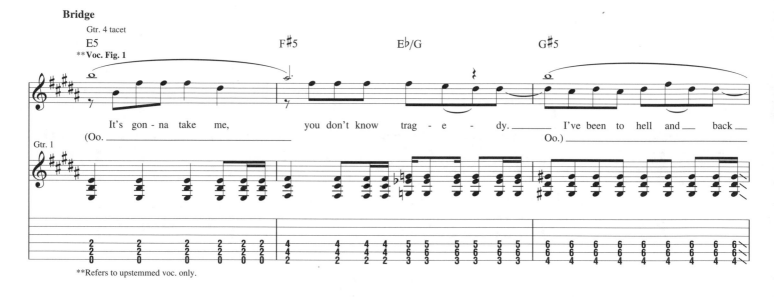

It's gon - na take me, ___ you don't know trag - e - dy. ___ I've been to hell and ___ back ___
(Oo. _____ Oo.) ___

Gtr. 1

**Refers to upstemmed voc. only.

Bkgd. Voc.: w/ Voc. Fig. 1

End Voc. Fig. 1

___ a - gain to tell and... Close my eyes and lay me down to ___ sleep. ___

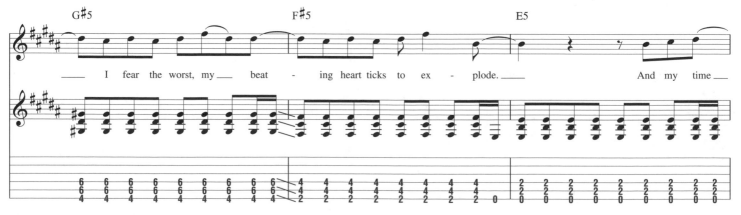

I fear the worst, my ___ beat - ing heart ticks to ex - plode. ___ And my time

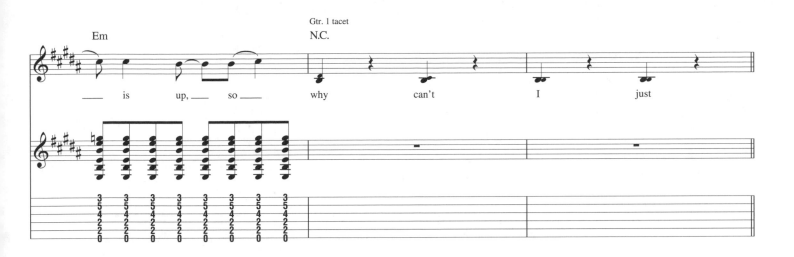

is up, ___ so ___ why   can't   I   just

Guitar Solo

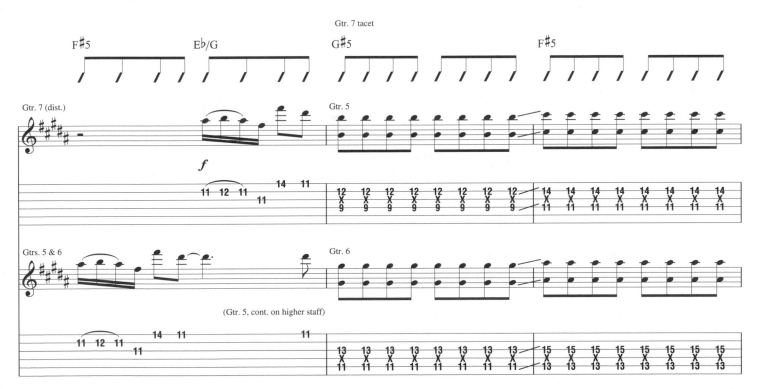

sleep? _____

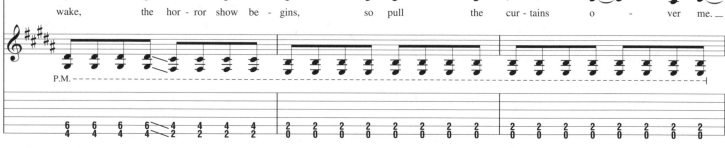

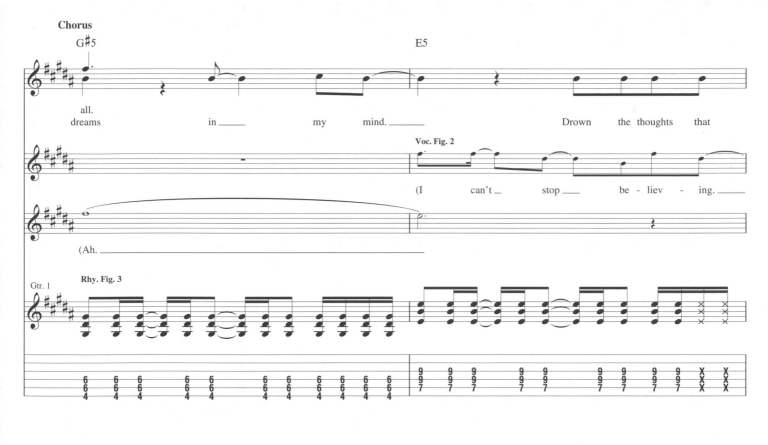

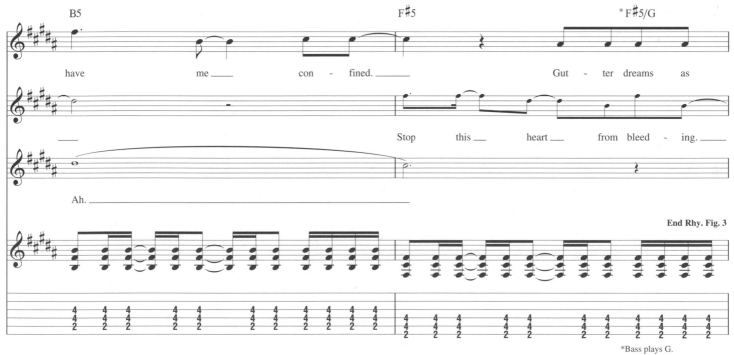

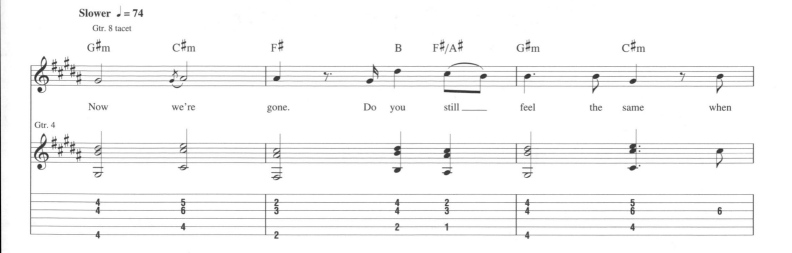

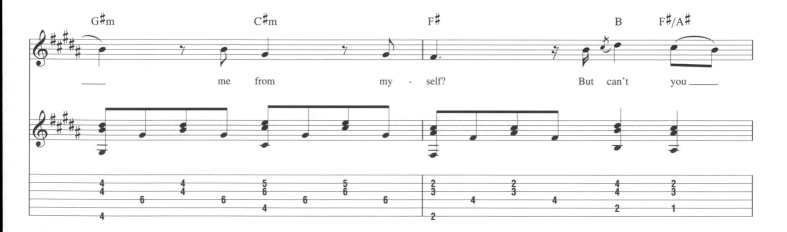

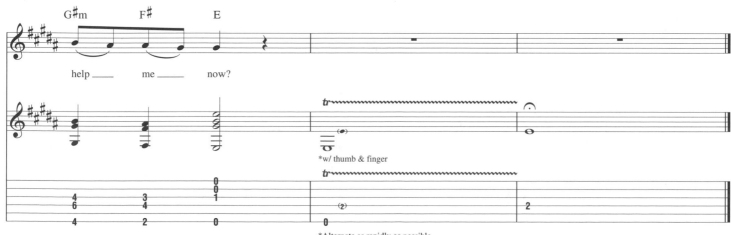

King of Contradiction

Words and Music by Deryck Whibley

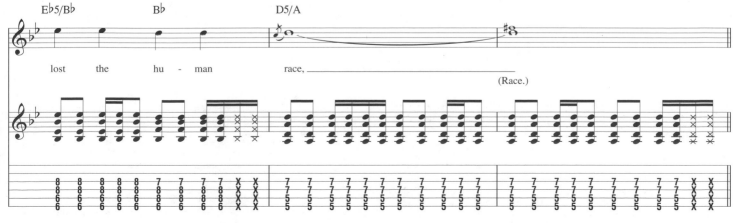

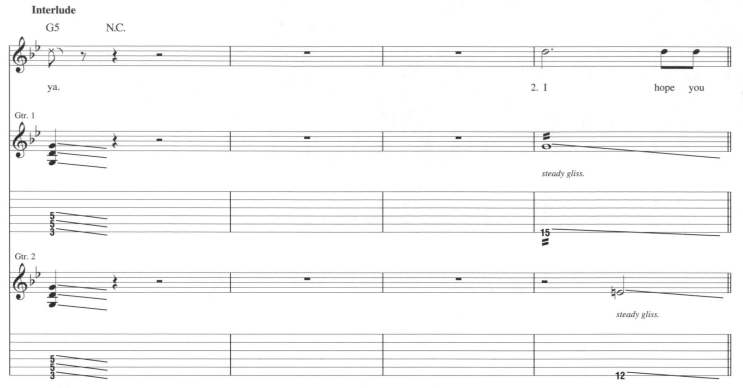

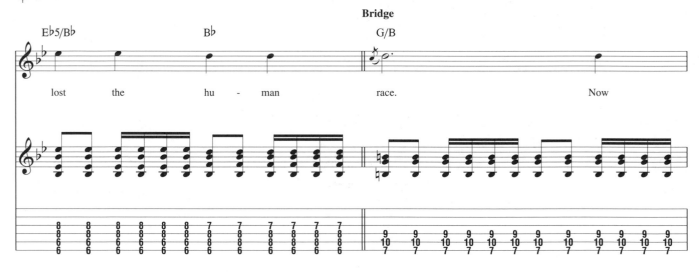

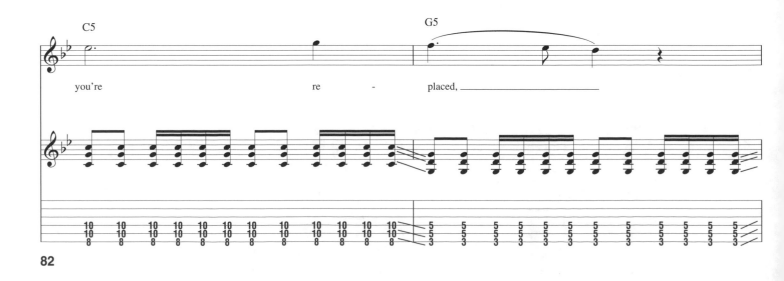

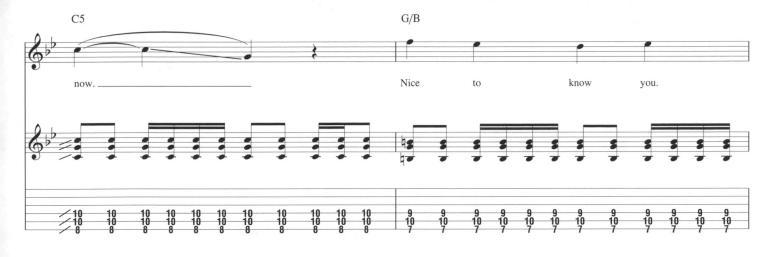

now. _____ Nice to know you.

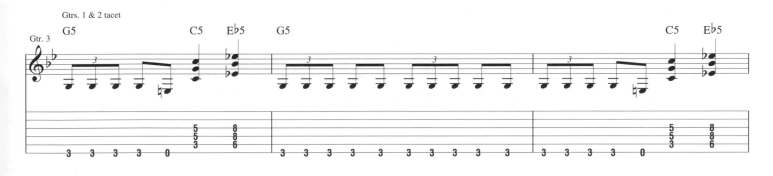

Outro
End double-time feel

Now your time is up so...

(cont. in slashes)

Gtr. 3 (dist.)

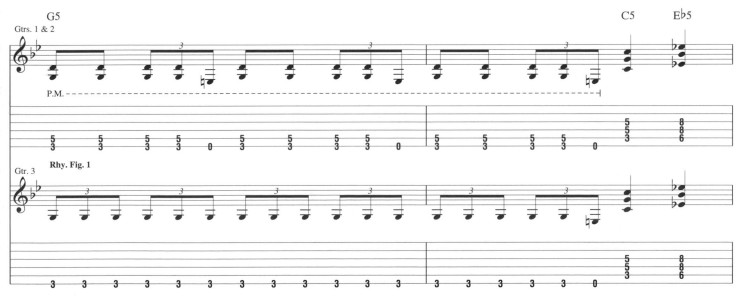

Gtrs. 1 & 2 tacet

Rhy. Fig. 1

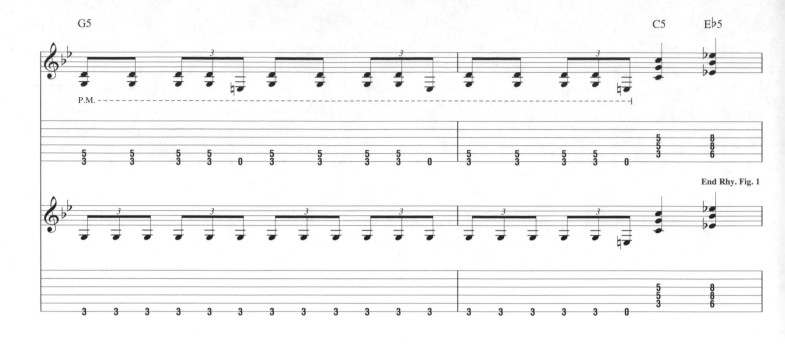

End Rhy. Fig. 1

Gtr. 3: w/ Rhy. Fig. 1

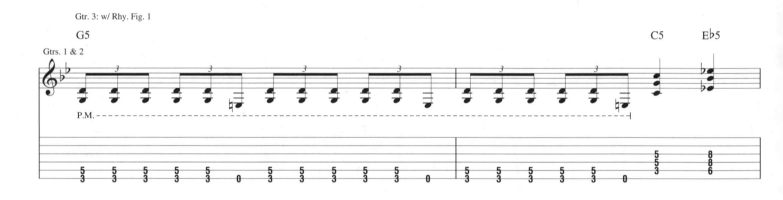

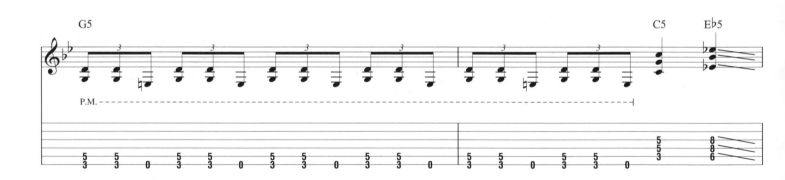

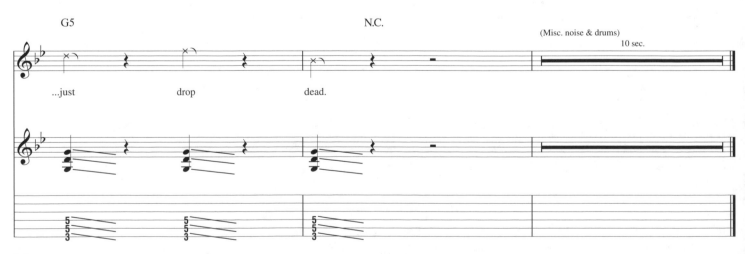

...just   drop   dead.

(Misc. noise & drums)
10 sec.

Best of Me

Words and Music by Deryck Whibley

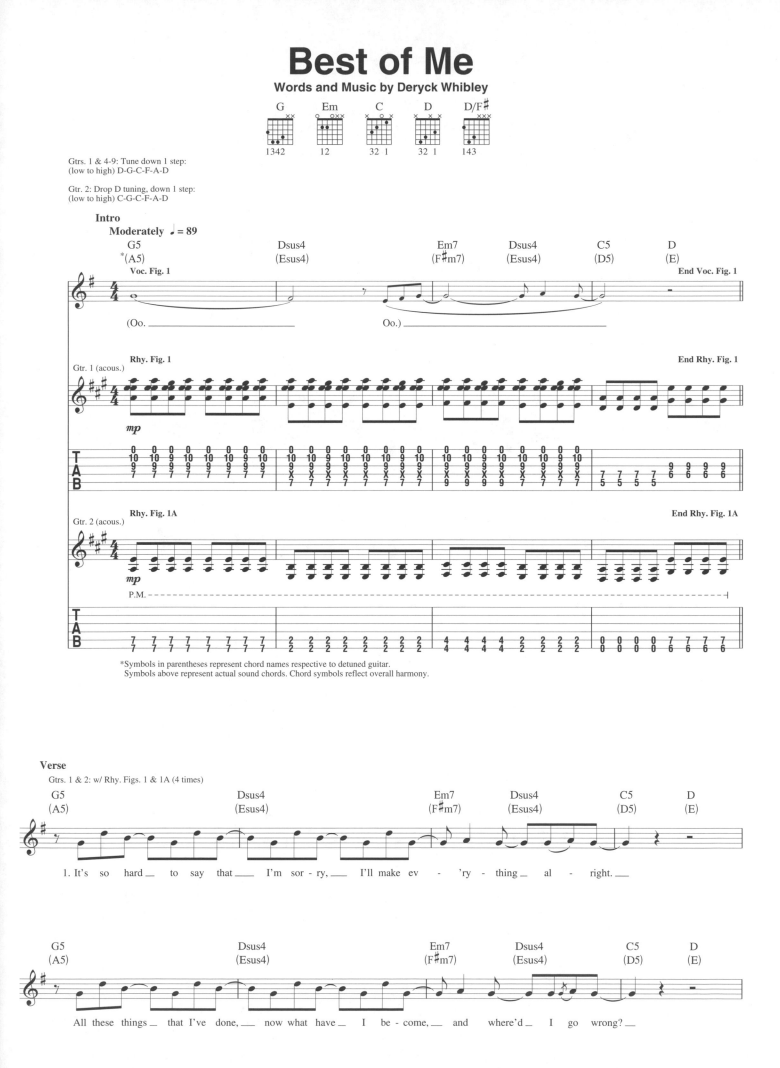

Bkgd. Voc.: w/ Voc. Fig. 1

I don't mean __ to hurt __ just to put __ you first. I won't tell __ you lies. __

(I'm sor - ry.) __

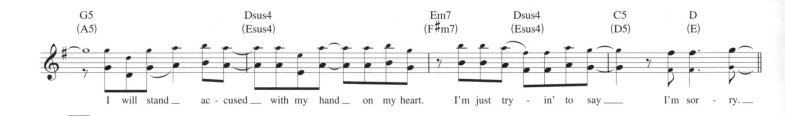

I will stand __ ac - cused __ with my hand __ on my heart. I'm just try - in' to say __ I'm sor - ry. __

Chorus

It's all that I can say. __ You

Rhy. Fig. 2

*Gtr. 3 (acous.)

*Doubled throughout

mean so much, __ and I'd fix all that I've done __ if I could __ start __ a - gain.

End Rhy. Fig. 2

Gtr. 3: w/ Rhy. Fig. 2

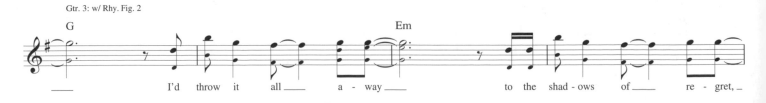

__ I'd throw it all __ a - way __ to the shad - ows of __ re - gret,

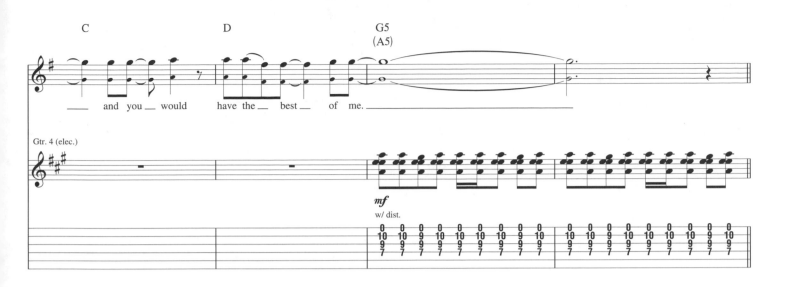

C   D   G5
                                          (A5)

and you ___ would ___ have the ___ best ___ of me. _____

Gtr. 4 (elec.)

mf
w/ dist.

Interlude

Bkgd. Voc.: w/ Voc. Fig. 1
Gtrs. 1 & 2: w/ Rhy. Figs. 1 & 1A

G5   Dsus4   Em7   Dsus4   Csus2   Dadd4
(A5)   (Esus4)   (F#m7)   (Esus4)   (Dsus2)   (Eadd4)

Rhy. Fig. 3   End Rhy. Fig. 3

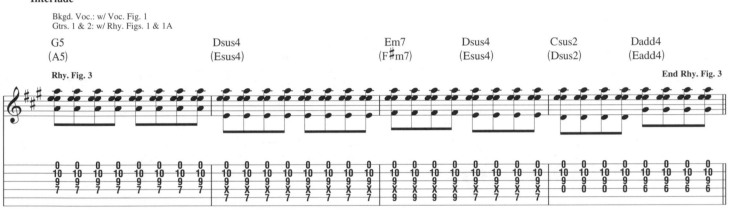

Verse

Gtrs. 1 & 2: w/ Rhy. Figs. 1 & 1A (4 times)
Gtr. 4: w/ Rhy. Fig. 3 (4 times)

G5   Dsus4   Em7   Dsus4   Csus2   Dadd4
(A5)   (Esus4)   (F#m7)   (Esus4)   (Dsus2)   (Eadd4)

2. I know that ___ I can't take ___ back all of ___ the mis-takes, ___ but I ____ will ___ try. ____

G5   Dsus4   Em7   Dsus4   Csus2   Dadd4
(A5)   (Esus4)   (F#m7)   (Esus4)   (Dsus2)   (Eadd4)

Al-though it's ___ not eas-y ___ I know you ___ be-lieve me, ___ 'cause I would ___ not ___ lie. ___

G5   Dsus4   Em7   Dsus4   Csus2   Dadd4
(A5)   (Esus4)   (F#m7)   (Esus4)   (Dsus2)   (Eadd4)

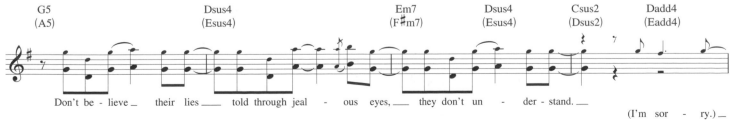

Don't be-lieve ___ their lies ___ told through jeal - ous eyes, ___ they don't un - der-stand. ___

(I'm sor - ry.)

I won't break __ your heart, __ I won't bring __ you down, __ but I will __ have to say __ I'm sor — ry.

*Gtr. 5 (elec.)

f
w/ dist.

*Doubled throughout

Chorus

Gtr. 3: w/ Rhy. Fig. 2 (2 times)

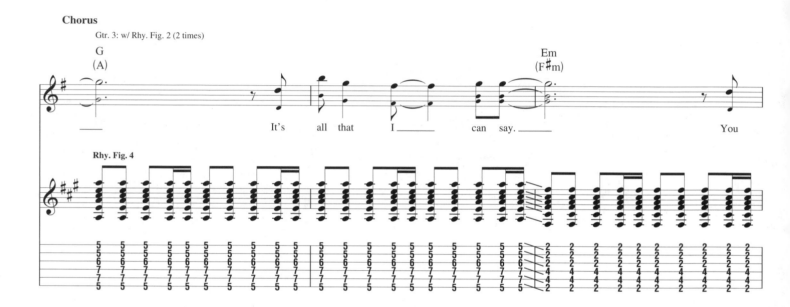

It's all that I __ can say. __ You

Rhy. Fig. 4

mean so much, __ and I'd fix all that I've done __ if I could __ start __ a — gain.

End Rhy. Fig. 4

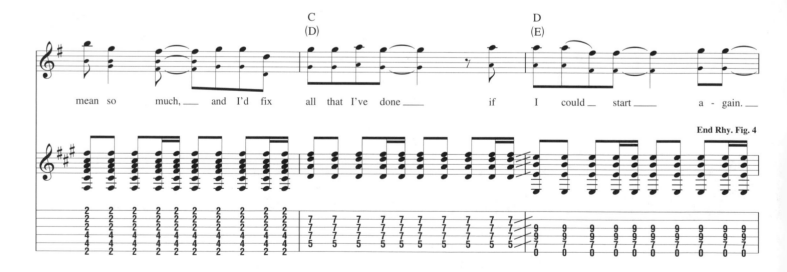

Gtr. 5: w/ Rhy. Fig. 4

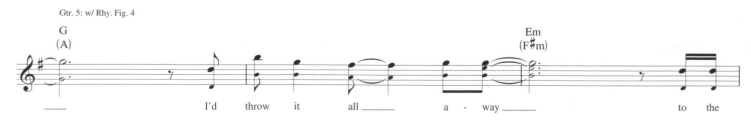

__ I'd throw it all __ a — way __ to the

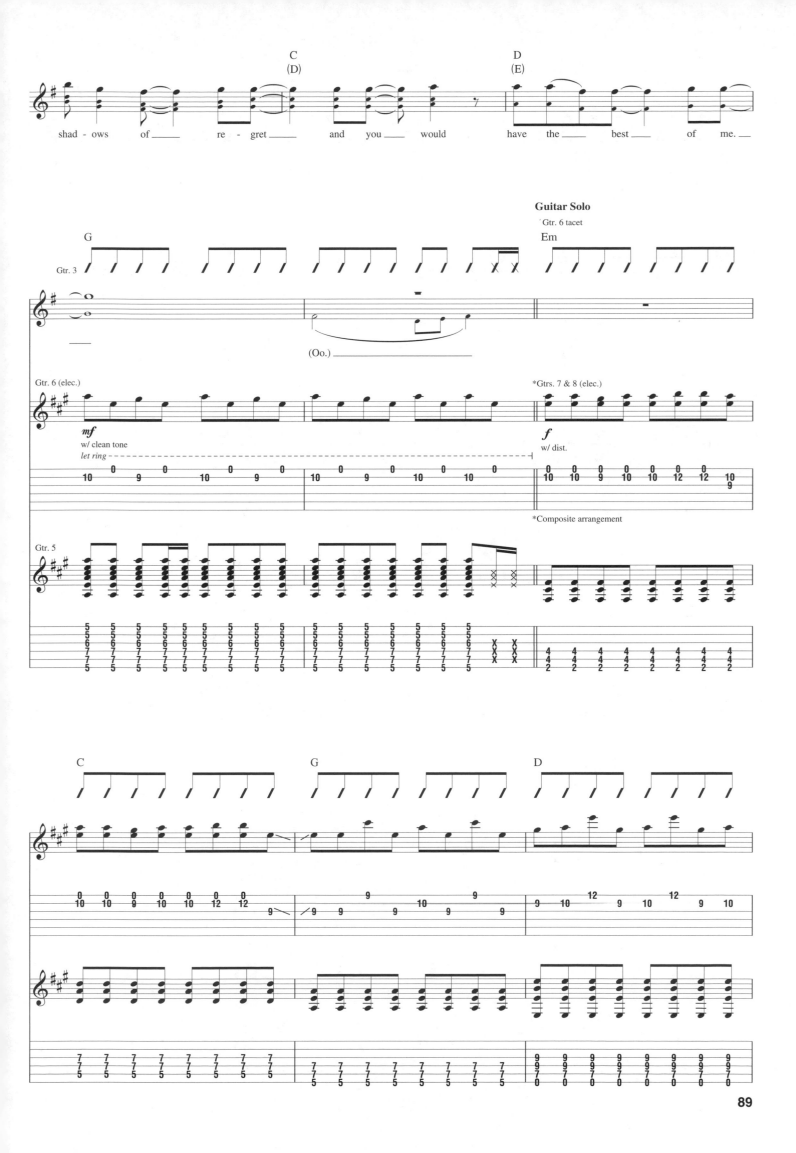

shad - ows   of ____   re - gret ____   and   you ____   would   have   the ____   best ____   of   me.

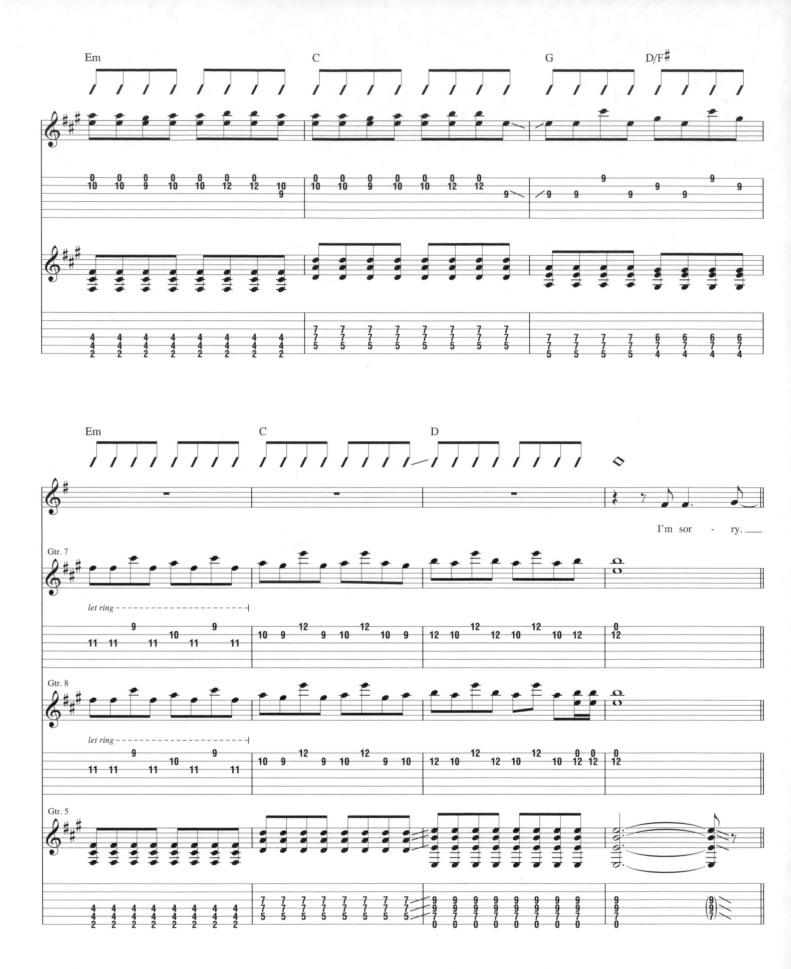

mean so much, ___ and I'd fix all that I've done ___ if I could ___ start ___ a - gain. ___

___ I'd throw it all ___ a - way ___ to the

shad - ows of ___ re - gret ___ and you ___ would have the ___ best ___ of me. ___

Play 5 times and fade

Outro

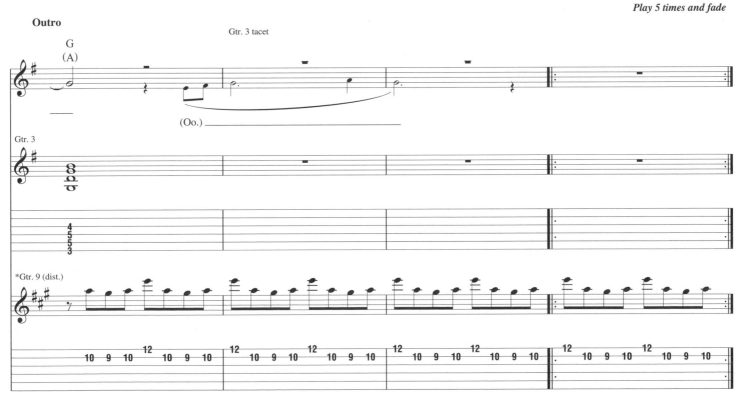

(Oo.) ___

*Bkwds. gtr. arr. for gtr.

Confusion and Frustration
in Modern Times

Words and Music by Deryck Whibley

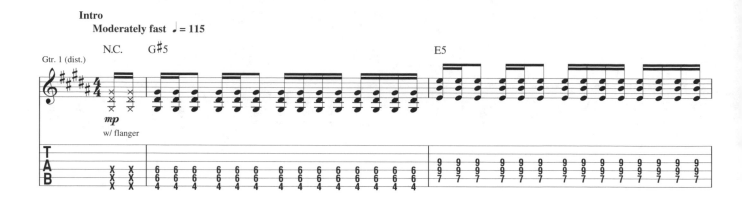

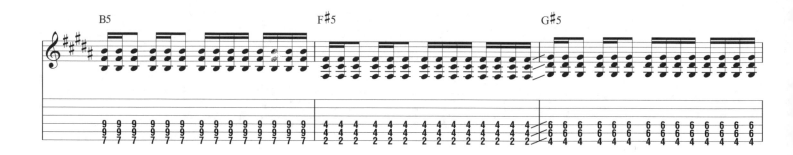

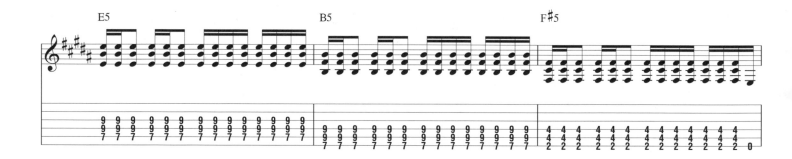

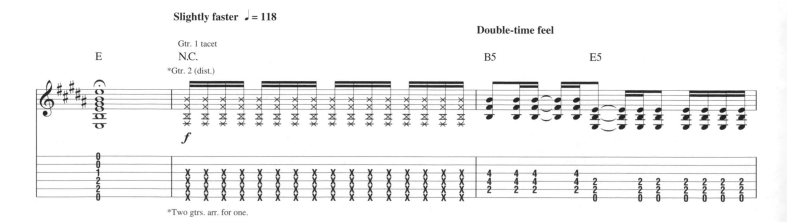

*Two gtrs. arr. for one.

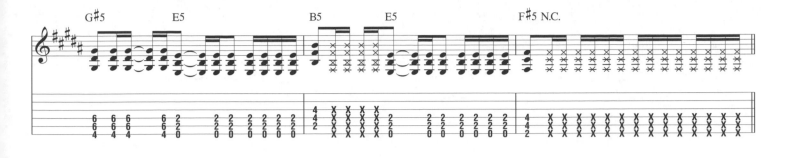

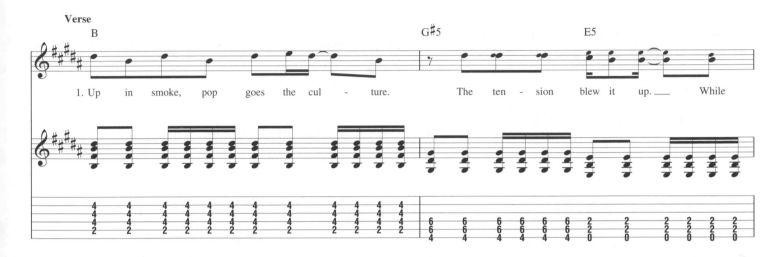

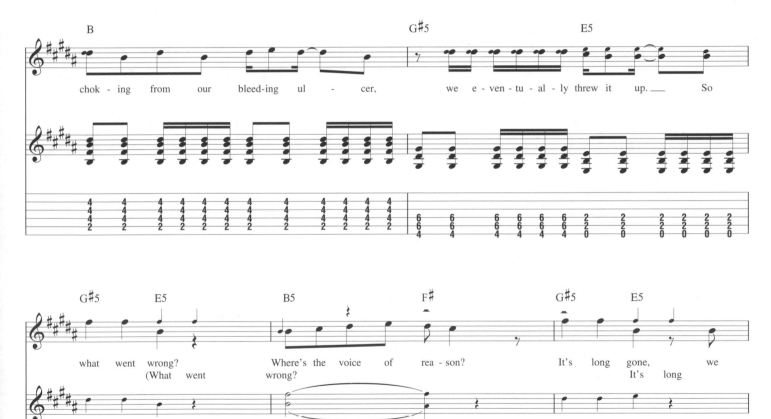

Verse

1. Up in smoke, pop goes the cul - ture. The ten - sion blew it up. ___ While

chok - ing from our bleed-ing ul - cer, we e - ven-tu - al -ly threw it up. ___ So

what went wrong? Where's the voice of rea - son? It's long gone, we
(What went wrong? It's long
(What went wrong? Ah. ___ It's long gone.

Rhy. Fig. 1

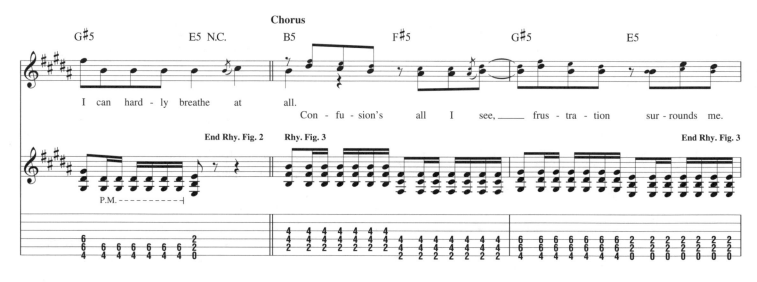

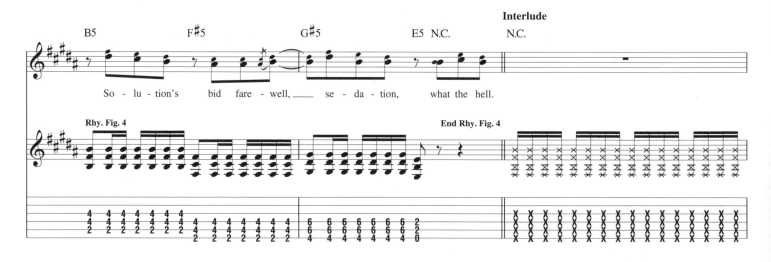

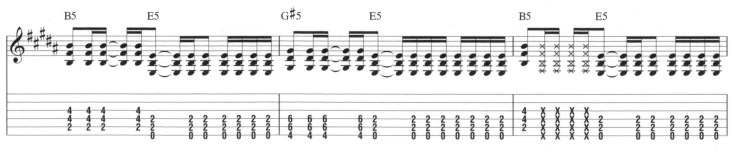

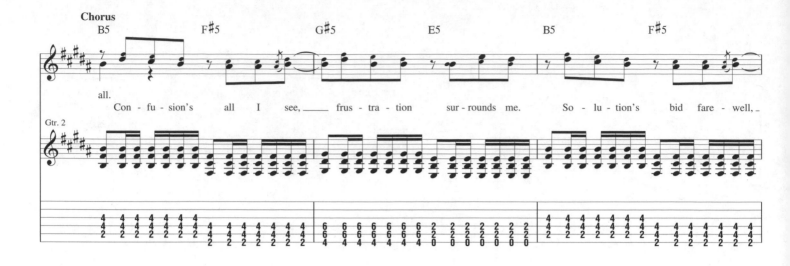

Chorus

all. Con - fu - sion's all I see,___ frus - tra - tion sur - rounds me. So - lu - tion's bid fare - well,___

Gtr. 2: w/ Rhy. Fig. 3

___ se - da - tion, what the hell. Con - fu - sion's all I see,___

Pitch: D#

*Harm. located approx. two-tenths the
distance between the 1st & 2nd frets.

Gtr. 2: w/ Rhy. Fig. 4

___ frus - tra - tion sur - rounds me. So - lu - tion's bid fare - well,___ se - da - tion, what the hell.

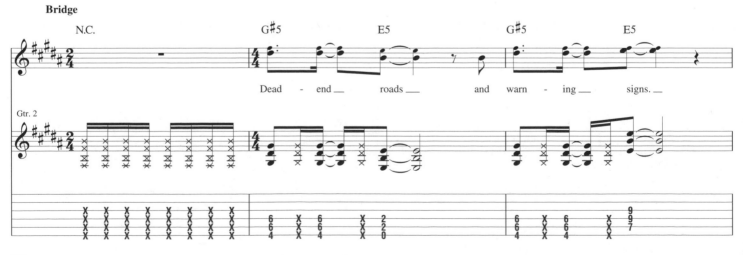

Bridge

Dead - end___ roads___ and warn - ing___ signs.___

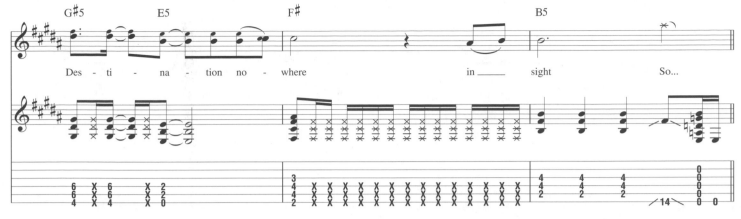

Des-ti-na-tion no-where   in ___ sight   So...

Interlude
Half-time feel

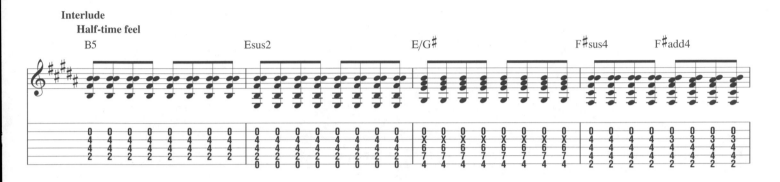

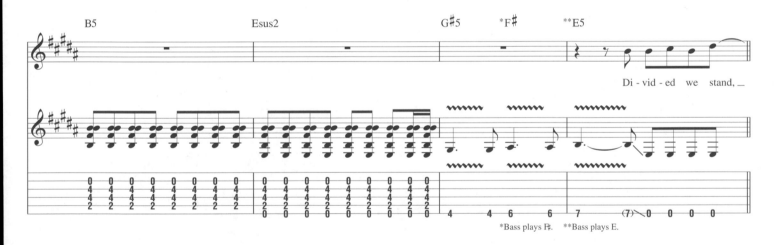

Di-vid-ed we stand, ___

*Bass plays F♯.   **Bass plays E.

Bridge

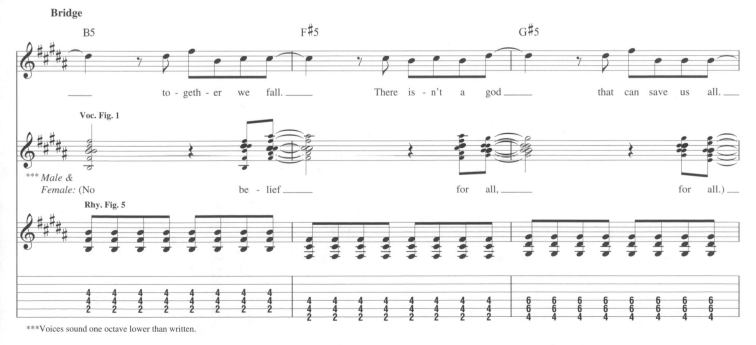

___ to-geth-er we fall. ___ There is-n't a god ___ that can save us all.

Voc. Fig. 1

*** *Male &*
Female: (No   be-lief ___   for   all, ___   for all.)

Rhy. Fig. 5

***Voices sound one octave lower than written.

So don't pray on your knees, _____ just beg on your hands. _____ There is no be - lief _____

End Voc. Fig. 1

End Rhy. Fig. 5

_____ in this prom - ised land. _____ Di - vid - ed we stand, _____ to - geth - er we fall. _____

_____ There's no _____ god _____ that can save us all. _____ So don't pray on your knees, _____

_____ just beg on your hands. _____ There is no be - lief _____ in this prom - ised land. _____ There is no be - lief. _____

Interlude

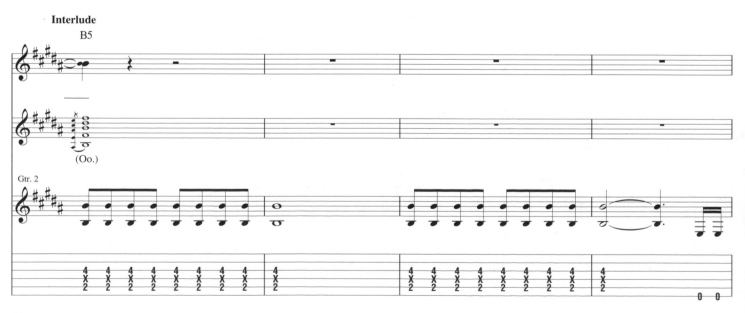

(Oo.)

Gtr. 2

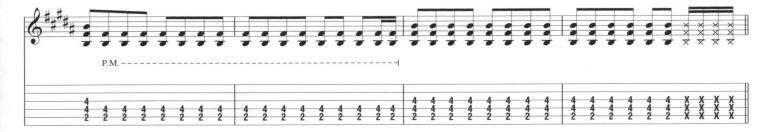

P.M. -

Chorus

Double-time feel

Gtr. 2: w/ Rhy. Fig. 3 (3 times)

B5   F#5   G#5   E5   B5   F#5

Con - fu - sion's   all   I   see, ___ frus - tra - tion   sur - rounds me.   So - lu - tion's   bid   fare - well, ___

G#5   E5   B5   F#5   G#5   E5

___ se - da - tion,   what   the   hell.   Con - fu - sion's   all   I   see, ___ frus - tra - tion   sur - rounds me.

Outro

B5   F#5   G#5   E5 N.C.   B5

So - lu - tion's   bid   fare - well, ___ se - da - tion,   what   the   hell.

Gtr. 3 (dist.)

Riff A1

f

Gtr. 2

Riff A

99

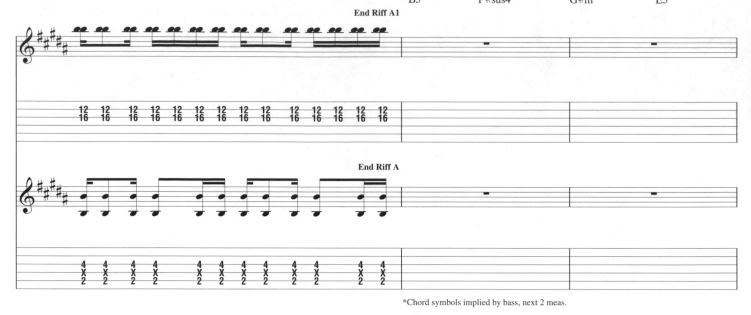

Gtrs. 2 & 3: w/ Riffs A & A1 (3 times)

*B5   F#sus4   G#m   E5

End Riff A1

End Riff A

*Chord symbols implied by bass, next 2 meas.

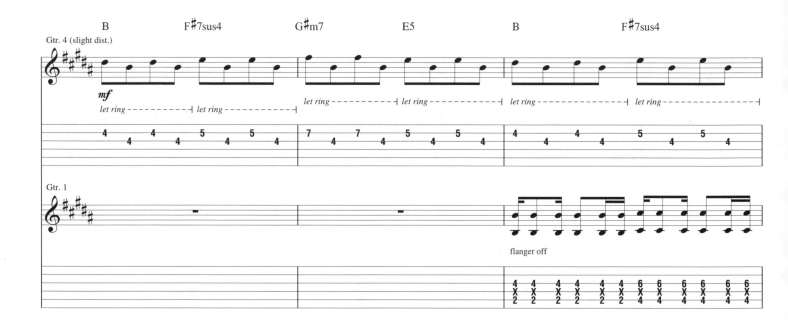

B   F#7sus4   G#m7   E5   B   F#7sus4

Gtr. 4 (slight dist.)

mf
let ring — — — — — | let ring — — — — — | let ring — — — — — | let ring — — — — — | let ring — — — — — | let ring — — — — —

Gtr. 1

flanger off

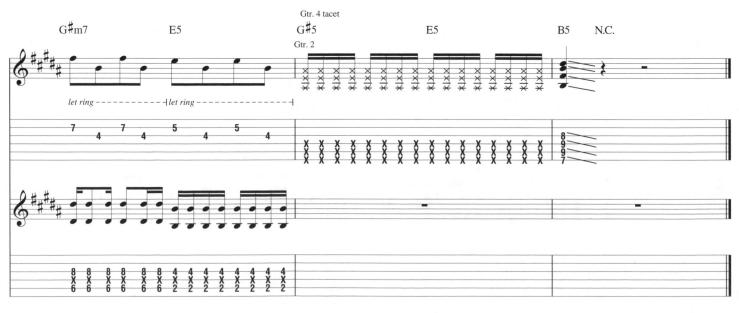

G#m7   E5   G#5   E5   B5   N.C.

Gtr. 4 tacet

Gtr. 2

let ring — — — — — | let ring — — — — —

So Long Goodbye

Words and Music by Deryck Whibley

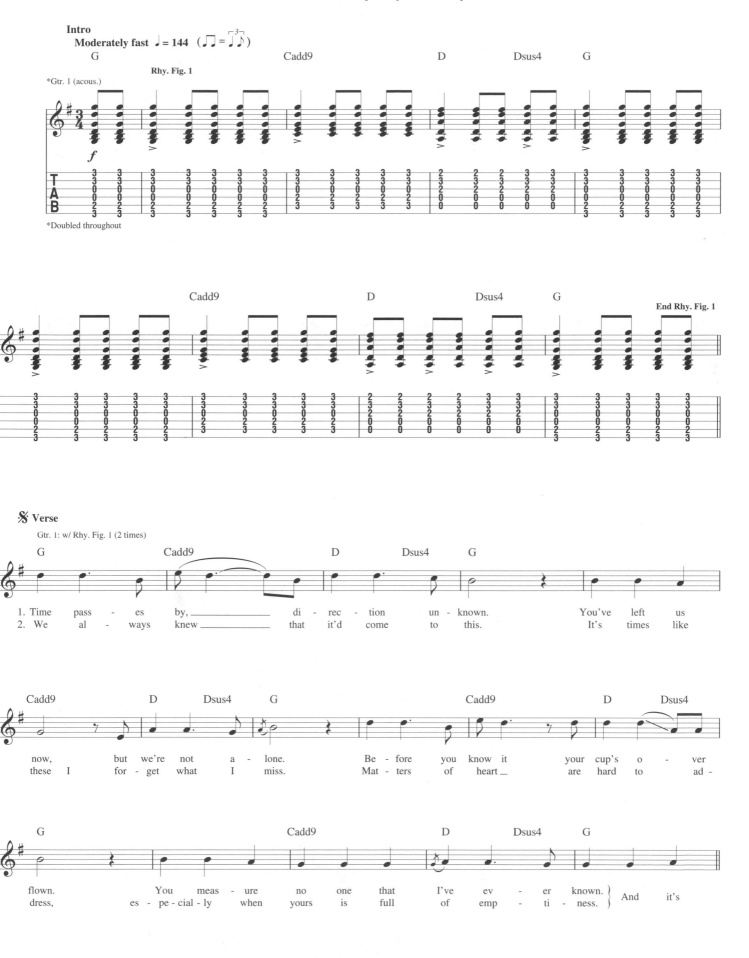

Chorus

quite _____ al - right. And good - bye _____

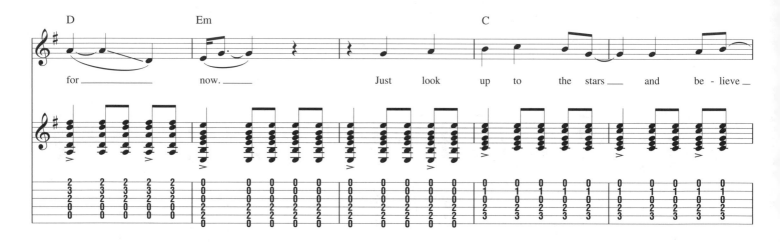

for _____ now. _____ Just look up to the stars ___ and be - lieve __

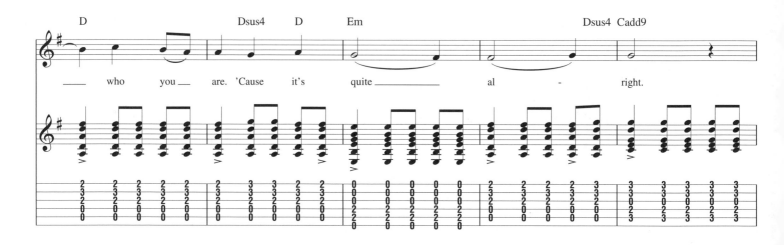

___ who you ___ are. 'Cause it's quite _____ al - right.

To Coda ⊕

Interlude

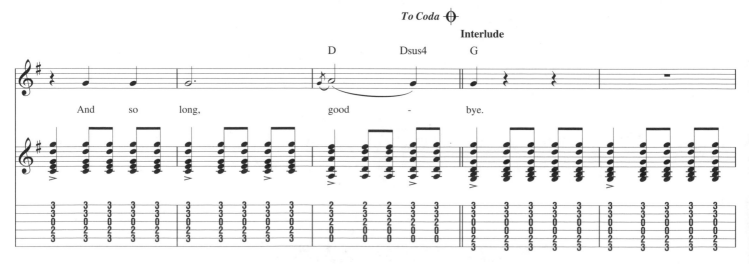

And so long, good - bye.

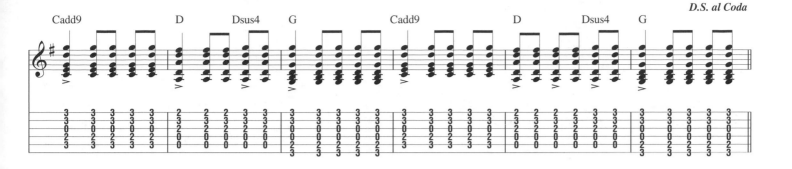

Coda

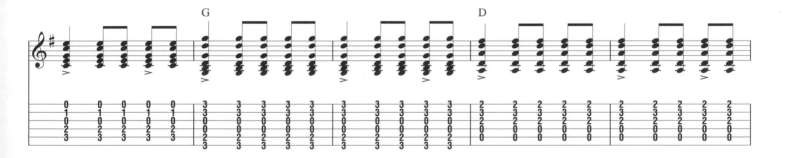

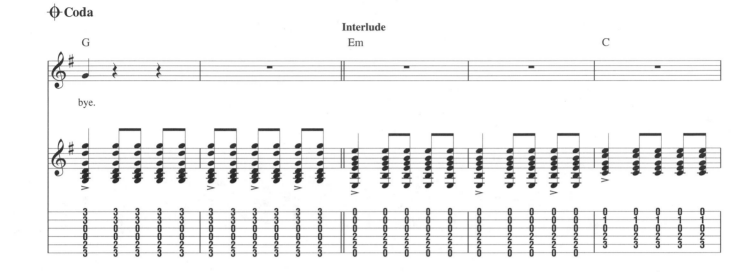

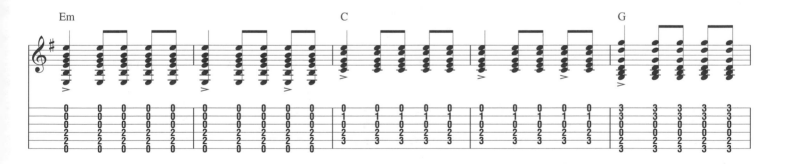

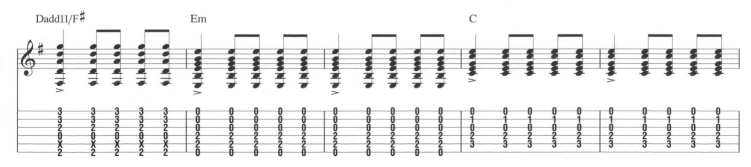

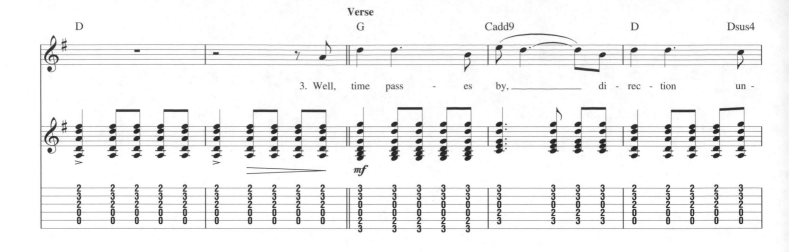

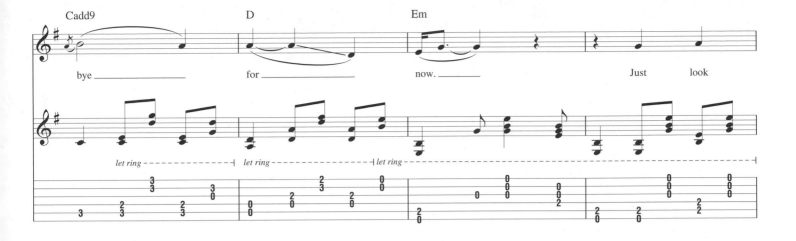

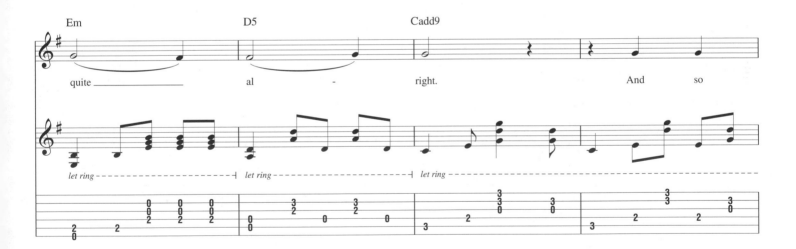

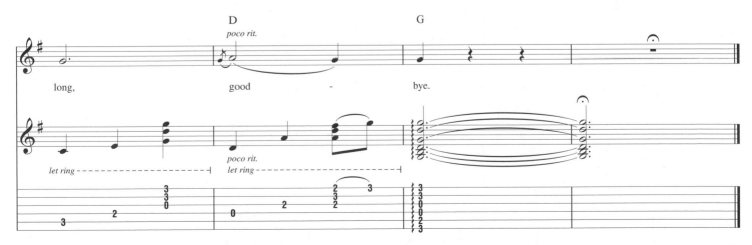

Look at Me

Words and Music by Deryck Whibley

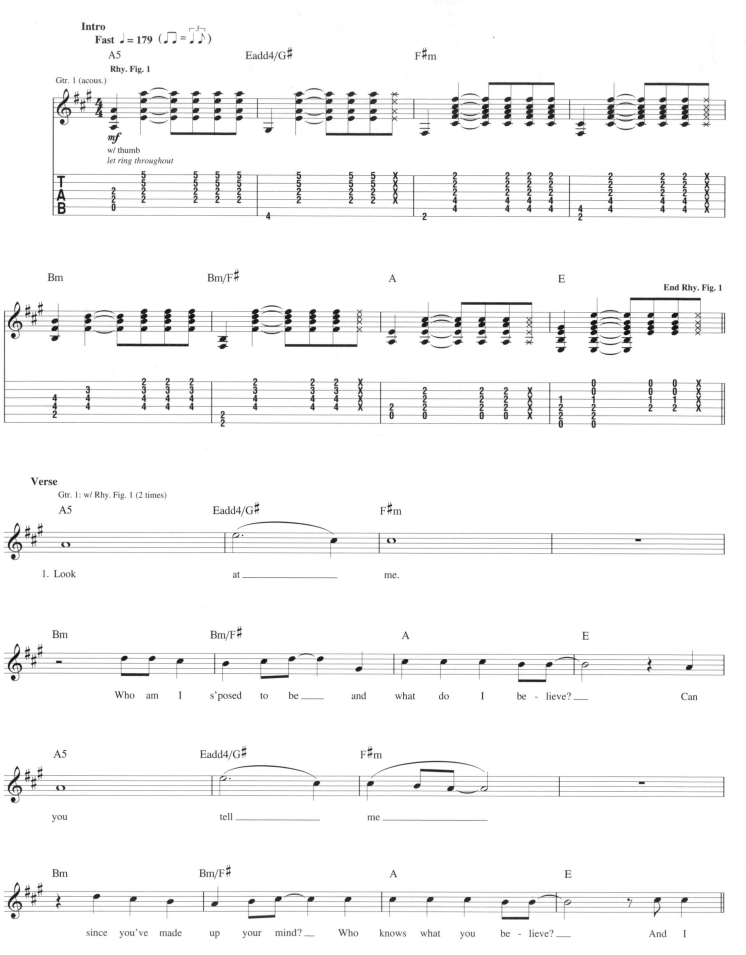

look ____ at ____ me.

Will I ev-er be ____ more than just a mem-o-ry? ____ 'Cause you

Chorus
Gtr. 1: w/ Riff A (4 times)
Gtr. 2: w/ Riff A1 (2 times)

just ____ don't ____ know.   No, you

just ____ don't ____ know. ____   All I am is

me. ____   All I am is

me. ____   All I am is

Outro

Begin fade

Gtr. 1: w/ Rhy. Fig. 1 (2 times)

me.

Fade out

Gtr. 1: w/ Riff A (till fade)

Guitar Notation Legend

Guitar music can be notated three different ways: on a *musical staff*, in *tablature*, and in *rhythm slashes*.

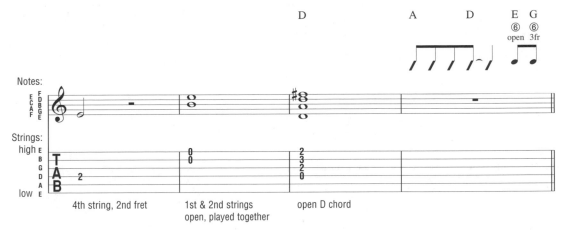

RHYTHM SLASHES are written above the staff. Strum chords in the rhythm indicated. Use the chord diagrams found at the top of the first page of the transcription for the appropriate chord voicings. Round noteheads indicate single notes.

THE MUSICAL STAFF shows pitches and rhythms and is divided by bar lines into measures. Pitches are named after the first seven letters of the alphabet.

TABLATURE graphically represents the guitar fingerboard. Each horizontal line represents a string, and each number represents a fret.

4th string, 2nd fret

1st & 2nd strings open, played together

open D chord

Definitions for Special Guitar Notation

HALF-STEP BEND: Strike the note and bend up 1/2 step.

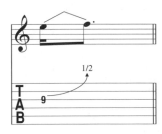

WHOLE-STEP BEND: Strike the note and bend up one step.

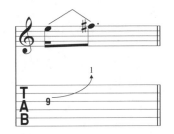

GRACE NOTE BEND: Strike the note and immediately bend up as indicated.

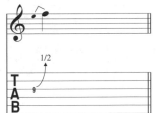

SLIGHT (MICROTONE) BEND: Strike the note and bend up 1/4 step.

BEND AND RELEASE: Strike the note and bend up as indicated, then release back to the original note. Only the first note is struck.

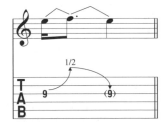

PRE-BEND: Bend the note as indicated, then strike it.

PRE-BEND AND RELEASE: Bend the note as indicated. Strike it and release the bend back to the original note.

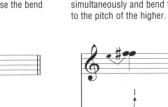

UNISON BEND: Strike the two notes simultaneously and bend the lower note up to the pitch of the higher.

VIBRATO: The string is vibrated by rapidly bending and releasing the note with the fretting hand.

WIDE VIBRATO: The pitch is varied to a greater degree by vibrating with the fretting hand.

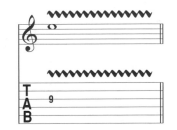

HAMMER-ON: Strike the first (lower) note with one finger, then sound the higher note (on the same string) with another finger by fretting it without picking.

PULL-OFF: Place both fingers on the notes to be sounded. Strike the first note and without picking, pull the finger off to sound the second (lower) note.

LEGATO SLIDE: Strike the first note and then slide the same fret-hand finger up or down to the second note. The second note is not struck.

SHIFT SLIDE: Same as legato slide, except the second note is struck.

TRILL: Very rapidly alternate between the notes indicated by continuously hammering on and pulling off.

TAPPING: Hammer ("tap") the fret indicated with the pick-hand index or middle finger and pull off to the note fretted by the fret hand.

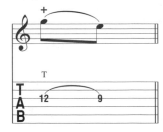

NATURAL HARMONIC: Strike the note while the fret-hand lightly touches the string directly over the fret indicated.

PINCH HARMONIC: The note is fretted normally and a harmonic is produced by adding the edge of the thumb or the tip of the index finger of the pick hand to the normal pick attack.

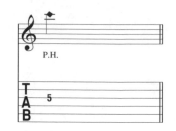

HARP HARMONIC: The note is fretted normally and a harmonic is produced by gently resting the pick hand's index finger directly above the indicated fret (in parentheses) while the pick hand's thumb or pick assists by plucking the appropriate string.

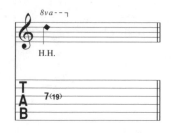

PICK SCRAPE: The edge of the pick is rubbed down (or up) the string, producing a scratchy sound.

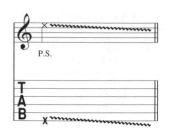

MUFFLED STRINGS: A percussive sound is produced by laying the fret hand across the string(s) without depressing, and striking them with the pick hand.

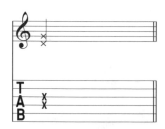

PALM MUTING: The note is partially muted by the pick hand lightly touching the string(s) just before the bridge.

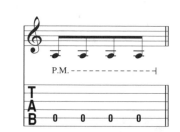

RAKE: Drag the pick across the strings indicated with a single motion.

TREMOLO PICKING: The note is picked as rapidly and continuously as possible.

ARPEGGIATE: Play the notes of the chord indicated by quickly rolling them from bottom to top.

VIBRATO BAR DIVE AND RETURN: The pitch of the note or chord is dropped a specified number of steps (in rhythm), then returned to the original pitch.

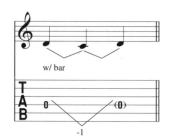

VIBRATO BAR SCOOP: Depress the bar just before striking the note, then quickly release the bar.

VIBRATO BAR DIP: Strike the note and then immediately drop a specified number of steps, then release back to the original pitch.

Additional Musical Definitions

> (accent)	• Accentuate note (play it louder).	
^ (accent)	• Accentuate note with great intensity.	
• (staccato)	• Play the note short.	
⊓	• Downstroke	
V	• Upstroke	
D.S. al Coda	• Go back to the sign (𝄋), then play until the measure marked "***To Coda***," then skip to the section labelled "**Coda**."	
D.C. al Fine	• Go back to the beginning of the song and play until the measure marked "***Fine***" (end).	

Rhy. Fig. • Label used to recall a recurring accompaniment pattern (usually chordal).

Riff • Label used to recall composed, melodic lines (usually single notes) which recur.

Fill • Label used to identify a brief melodic figure which is to be inserted into the arrangement.

Rhy. Fill • A chordal version of a Fill.

tacet • Instrument is silent (drops out).

• Repeat measures between signs.

• When a repeated section has different endings, play the first ending only the first time and the second ending only the second time.

NOTE: Tablature numbers in parentheses mean:
    1. The note is being sustained over a system (note in standard notation is tied), or
    2. The note is sustained, but a new articulation (such as a hammer-on, pull-off, slide or vibrato) begins, or
    3. The note is a barely audible "ghost" note (note in standard notation is also in parentheses).

RECORDED VERSIONS®
The Best Note-For-Note Transcriptions Available

ALL BOOKS INCLUDE TABLATURE

00692015 Aerosmith – Greatest Hits......................$22.95	00692931 Jimi Hendrix – Axis: Bold As Love..............$22.95	00694975 Queen – Greatest Hits $24.95
00690603 Aerosmith – O Yeah! (Ultimate Hits) $24.95	00690608 Jimi Hendrix – Blue Wild Angel....................$24.95	00690670 Queensryche – Very Best of.......................$19.95
00690178 Alice in Chains – Acoustic $19.95	00692932 Jimi Hendrix – Electric Ladyland....................$24.95	00690878 The Raconteurs – Broken Boy Soldiers $19.95
00694865 Alice in Chains – Dirt..............................$19.95	00690017 Jimi Hendrix – Live at Woodstock................$24.95	00694910 Rage Against the Machine..........................$19.95
00690387 Alice in Chains – Nothing Safe:	00690602 Jimi Hendrix – Smash Hits $19.95	00690055 Red Hot Chili Peppers –
The Best of the Box $19.95	00690843 H.I.M. – Dark Light $19.95	Blood Sugar Sex Magik $19.95
00690812 All American Rejects – Move Along $19.95	00690869 Hinder – Extreme Behavior $19.95	00690584 Red Hot Chili Peppers – By the Way $19.95
00694932 Allman Brothers Band – Volume 1 ....$24.95	00690692 Billy Idol – Very Best of.............................$19.95	00690379 Red Hot Chili Peppers – Californication $19.95
00694933 Allman Brothers Band – Volume 2 ....$24.95	00690688 Incubus – A Crow Left of the Murder $19.95	00690673 Red Hot Chili Peppers – Greatest Hits $19.95
00694934 Allman Brothers Band – Volume 3 ....$24.95	00690457 Incubus – Make Yourself $19.95	00690852 Red Hot Chili Peppers –
00690865 Atreyu – A Deathgrip on Yesterday $19.95	00690544 Incubus – Morningview $19.95	Stadium Arcadium $24.95
00690609 Audioslave..$19.95	00690790 Iron Maiden Anthology $24.95	00690511 Django Reinhardt – Definitive Collection....$19.95
00690804 Audioslave – Out of Exile $19.95	00690730 Alan Jackson – Guitar Collection $19.95	00690779 Relient K – MMHMM...............................$19.95
00690884 Audioslave – Revelations $19.95	00690721 Jet – Get Born $19.95	00690643 Relient K – Two Lefts Don't
00690820 Avenged Sevenfold – City of Evil $22.95	00690684 Jethro Tull – Aqualung $19.95	Make a Right...But Three Do $19.95
00690366 Bad Company – Original Anthology,	00690647 Jewel – Best of $19.95	00690631 Rolling Stones – Guitar Anthology $24.95
Book 1 ....$19.95	00690814 John5 – Songs for Sanity $19.95	00690685 David Lee Roth – Eat 'Em and Smile...........$19.95
00690503 Beach Boys – Very Best of $19.95	00690751 John5 – Vertigo $19.95	00690694 David Lee Roth – Guitar Anthology.............$24.95
00690489 Beatles – 1 ....$24.95	00690845 Eric Johnson – Bloom $19.95	00690031 Santana's Greatest Hits $19.95
00694929 Beatles – 1962-1966..$24.95	00690846 Jack Johnson and Friends – Sing-A-Longs and	00690796 Michael Schenker – Very Best of................$19.95
00694930 Beatles – 1967-1970..$24.95	Lullabies for the Film Curious George $19.95	00690566 Scorpions – Best of...................................$19.95
00694832 Beatles – For Acoustic Guitar $22.95	00690271 Robert Johnson – New Transcriptions........$24.95	00690604 Bob Seger – Guitar Collection $19.95
00690110 Beatles – White Album (Book 1) $19.95	00699131 Janis Joplin – Best of.................................$19.95	00690803 Kenny Wayne Shepherd Band – Best of $19.95
00692385 Chuck Berry $19.95	00690427 Judas Priest – Best of.................................$19.95	00690857 Shinedown – Us and Them $19.95
00690835 Billy Talent $19.95	00690742 The Killers – Hot Fuss $19.95	00690530 Slipknot – Iowa...$19.95
00692200 Black Sabbath –	00694903 Kiss – Best of $24.95	00690733 Slipknot – Vol. 3 (The Subliminal Verses)..$19.95
We Sold Our Soul for Rock 'N' Roll............$19.95	00690780 Korn – Greatest Hits, Volume 1 ....$22.95	00120004 Steely Dan – Best of $24.95
00690674 blink-182..$19.95	00690834 Lamb of God – Ashes of the Wake $19.95	00694921 Steppenwolf – Best of.................................$22.95
00690831 blink-182 – Greatest Hits $19.95	00690875 Lamb of God – Sacrament $19.95	00690655 Mike Stern – Best of...................................$19.95
00690491 David Bowie – Best of $19.95	00690823 Ray LaMontagne – Trouble $19.95	00690877 Stone Sour – Come What(ever) May $19.95
00690873 Breaking Benjamin – Phobia $19.95	00690679 John Lennon – Guitar Collection $19.95	00690520 Styx Guitar Collection $19.95
00690764 Breaking Benjamin – We Are Not Alone $19.95	00690781 Linkin Park – Hybrid Theory.......................$22.95	00120081 Sublime...$19.95
00690451 Jeff Buckley – Collection $24.95	00690782 Linkin Park – Meteora $22.95	00690771 SUM 41 – Chuck $19.95
00690590 Eric Clapton – Anthology..............................$29.95	00690783 Live – Best of $19.95	00690767 Switchfoot – The Beautiful Letdown $19.95
00690415 Clapton Chronicles – Best of Eric Clapton ..$18.95	00690743 Los Lonely Boys $19.95	00690830 System of a Down – Hypnotize $19.95
00690074 Eric Clapton – The Cream of Clapton $24.95	00690876 Los Lonely Boys – Sacred $19.95	00690799 System of a Down – Mezmerize $19.95
00690716 Eric Clapton – Me and Mr. Johnson $19.95	00690720 Lostprophets – Start Something..................$19.95	00690531 System of a Down – Toxicity $19.95
00694869 Eric Clapton – Unplugged $22.95	00694954 Lynyrd Skynyrd – New Best of $19.95	00694824 James Taylor – Best of................................$16.95
00690162 The Clash – Best of $19.95	00690752 Lynyrd Skynyrd – Street Survivors $19.95	00690871 Three Days Grace – One-X $19.95
00690828 Coheed & Cambria – Good Apollo I'm Burning	00690577 Yngwie Malmsteen – Anthology..................$24.95	00690737 3 Doors Down – The Better Life...................$22.95
Star, IV, Vol. 1: From Fear Through the	00690754 Marilyn Manson – Lest We Forget $19.95	00690683 Robin Trower – Bridge of Sighs $19.95
Eyes of Madness $19.95	00694956 Bob Marley– Legend $19.95	00690740 Shania Twain – Guitar Collection................$19.95
00690593 Coldplay – A Rush of Blood to the Head.....$19.95	00694945 Bob Marley– Songs of Freedom $24.95	00699191 U2 – Best of: 1980-1990 ....$19.95
00690838 Cream – Royal Albert Hall:	00690657 Maroon5 – Songs About Jane $19.95	00690732 U2 – Best of: 1990-2000 ....$19.95
London May 2-3-5-6 2005 ....$22.95	00120080 Don McLean – Songbook............................$19.95	00690775 U2 – How to Dismantle an Atomic Bomb ..$22.95
00690856 Creed – Greatest Hits $22.95	00694951 Megadeth – Rust in Peace $22.95	00690575 Steve Vai – Alive in an Ultra World $22.95
00690401 Creed – Human Clay $19.95	00690768 Megadeth – The System Has Failed..............$19.95	00660137 Steve Vai – Passion & Warfare $24.95
00690819 Creedence Clearwater Revival – Best of......$19.95	00690505 John Mellencamp – Guitar Collection..........$19.95	00690116 Stevie Ray Vaughan – Guitar Collection.......$24.95
00690572 Steve Cropper – Soul Man..............................$19.95	00690646 Pat Metheny – One Quiet Night..................$19.95	00660058 Stevie Ray Vaughan –
00690613 Crosby, Stills & Nash – Best of $19.95	00690558 Pat Metheny – Trio: 99>00 ....$19.95	Lightnin' Blues 1983-1987 ....$24.95
00690289 Deep Purple – Best of $17.95	00690040 Steve Miller Band – Young Hearts $19.95	00694835 Stevie Ray Vaughan – The Sky Is Crying $22.95
00690784 Def Leppard – Best of $19.95	00690794 Mudvayne – Lost and Found........................$19.95	00690015 Stevie Ray Vaughan – Texas Flood $19.95
00690347 The Doors – Anthology...................................$22.95	00690611 Nirvana...$22.95	00690772 Velvet Revolver – Contraband.....................$22.95
00690348 The Doors – Essential Guitar Collection $16.95	00694883 Nirvana – Nevermind $19.95	00690071 Weezer (The Blue Album) $19.95
00690810 Fall Out Boy – From Under the Cork Tree ..$19.95	00690026 Nirvana – Unplugged in New York $19.95	00690447 The Who – Best of......................................$24.95
00690664 Fleetwood Mac – Best of $19.95	00690807 The Offspring – Greatest Hits $19.95	00690589 ZZ Top Guitar Anthology............................$22.95
00690870 Flyleaf $19.95	00694847 Ozzy Osbourne – Best of $22.95	
00690808 Foo Fighters – In Your Honor $19.95	00690399 Ozzy Osbourne – Ozzman Cometh...............$19.95	
00690805 Robben Ford – Best of $19.95	00690866 Panic! At the Disco –	
00694920 Free – Best of $19.95	A Fever You Can't Sweat Out $19.95	
00690848 Godsmack – IV $19.95	00694855 Pearl Jam – Ten $19.95	
00690601 Good Charlotte –	00690439 A Perfect Circle – Mer De Noms $19.95	
The Young and the Hopeless $19.95	00690661 A Perfect Circle – Thirteenth Step...............$19.95	
00690697 Jim Hall – Best of..$19.95	00690499 Tom Petty – Definitive Guitar Collection $19.95	
00690840 Ben Harper – Both Sides of the Gun $19.95	00690428 Pink Floyd – Dark Side of the Moon..............$19.95	
00694798 George Harrison – Anthology..........................$19.95	00690789 Poison – Best of...$19.95	
00692930 Jimi Hendrix – Are You Experienced?..........$24.95	00693864 The Police – Best of....................................$19.95	

GUITAR *signature licks*

Signature Licks book/CD packs provide a step-by-step breakdown of "right from the record" riffs, licks, and solos so you can jam along with your favorite bands. They contain performance notes and an overview of each artist's or group's style, with note-for-note transcriptions in notes and tab. The CDs feature full-band demos at both normal and slow speeds.

BEST OF ACOUSTIC GUITAR
00695640 ....$19.95

AEROSMITH 1973-1979
00695106 ....$22.95

AEROSMITH 1979-1998
00695219 ....$22.95

BEST OF AGGRO-METAL
00695592 ....$19.95

BEST OF CHET ATKINS
00695752 ....$22.95

THE BEACH BOYS DEFINITIVE COLLECTION
00695683 ....$22.95

BEST OF THE BEATLES FOR ACOUSTIC GUITAR
00695453 ....$22.95

THE BEATLES BASS
00695283 ....$22.95

THE BEATLES FAVORITES
00695096 ....$24.95

THE BEATLES HITS
00695049 ....$24.95

BEST OF GEORGE BENSON
00695418 ....$22.95

BEST OF BLACK SABBATH
00695249 ....$22.95

BEST OF BLINK - 182
00695704 ....$22.95

BEST OF BLUES GUITAR
00695846 ....$19.95

BLUES GUITAR CLASSICS
00695177 ....$19.95

BLUES/ROCK GUITAR MASTERS
00695348 ....$19.95

BEST OF CHARLIE CHRISTIAN
00695584 ....$22.95

BEST OF ERIC CLAPTON
00695038 ....$24.95

ERIC CLAPTON – THE BLUESMAN
00695040 ....$22.95

ERIC CLAPTON – FROM THE ALBUM UNPLUGGED
00695250 ....$24.95

BEST OF CREAM
00695251 ....$22.95

DEEP PURPLE – GREATEST HITS
00695625 ....$22.95

THE BEST OF DEF LEPPARD
00696516 ....$22.95

THE DOORS
00695373 ....$22.95

FAMOUS ROCK GUITAR SOLOS
00695590 ....$19.95

BEST OF FOO FIGHTERS
00695481 ....$22.95

GREATEST GUITAR SOLOS OF ALL TIME
00695301 ....$19.95

BEST OF GRANT GREEN
00695747 ....$22.95

GUITAR INSTRUMENTAL HITS
00695309 ....$19.95

GUITAR RIFFS OF THE '60S
00695218 ....$19.95

BEST OF GUNS N' ROSES
00695183 ....$22.95

HARD ROCK SOLOS
00695591 ....$19.95

JIMI HENDRIX
00696560 ....$24.95

HOT COUNTRY GUITAR
00695580 ....$19.95

BEST OF JAZZ GUITAR
00695586 ....$24.95

ERIC JOHNSON
00699317 ....$22.95

ROBERT JOHNSON
00695264 ....$22.95

THE ESSENTIAL ALBERT KING
00695713 ....$22.95

B.B. KING – THE DEFINITIVE COLLECTION
00695635 ....$22.95

THE KINKS
00695553 ....$22.95

BEST OF KISS
00699413 ....$22.95

MARK KNOPFLER
00695178 ....$22.95

BEST OF YNGWIE MALMSTEEN
00695669 ....$22.95

BEST OF PAT MARTINO
00695632 ....$22.95

MEGADETH
00695041 ....$22.95

WES MONTGOMERY
00695387 ....$22.95

BEST OF NIRVANA
00695483 ....$24.95

THE OFFSPRING
00695852 ....$24.95

VERY BEST OF OZZY OSBOURNE
00695431 ....$22.95

BEST OF JOE PASS
00695730 ....$22.95

PINK FLOYD – EARLY CLASSICS
00695566 ....$22.95

THE POLICE
00695724 ....$22.95

THE GUITARS OF ELVIS
00696507 ....$22.95

BEST OF QUEEN
00695097 ....$22.95

BEST OF RAGE AGAINST THE MACHINE
00695480 ....$22.95

RED HOT CHILI PEPPERS
00695173 ....$22.95

RED HOT CHILI PEPPERS – GREATEST HITS
00695828 ....$24.95

BEST OF DJANGO REINHARDT
00695660 ....$22.95

BEST OF ROCK
00695884 ....$19.95

BEST OF ROCK 'N' ROLL GUITAR
00695559 ....$19.95

BEST OF ROCKABILLY GUITAR
00695785 ....$19.95

THE ROLLING STONES
00695079 ....$22.95

BEST OF JOE SATRIANI
00695216 ....$22.95

BEST OF SILVERCHAIR
00695488 ....$22.95

THE BEST OF SOUL GUITAR
00695703 ....$19.95

BEST OF SOUTHERN ROCK
00695703 ....$19.95

ROD STEWART
00695663 ....$22.95

BEST OF SYSTEM OF A DOWN
00695788 ....$22.95

STEVE VAI
00673247 ....$22.95

STEVE VAI – ALIEN LOVE SECRETS: THE NAKED VAMPS
00695223 ....$22.95

STEVE VAI – FIRE GARDEN: THE NAKED VAMPS
00695166 ....$22.95

STEVE VAI – THE ULTRA ZONE: NAKED VAMPS
00695684 ....$22.95

STEVIE RAY VAUGHAN
00699316 ....$24.95

THE GUITAR STYLE OF STEVIE RAY VAUGHAN
00695155 ....$24.95

BEST OF THE VENTURES
00695772 ....$19.95

THE WHO
00695561 ....$22.95

BEST OF ZZ TOP
00695738 ....$22.95

Complete descriptions and songlists online!

FOR MORE INFORMATION, SEE YOUR LOCAL MUSIC DEALER, OR WRITE TO:

HAL•LEONARD® CORPORATION
7777 W. BLUEMOUND RD. P.O. BOX 13819 MILWAUKEE, WI 53213

www.halleonard.com

Prices, contents and availability subject to change without notice.

0606